WOMEN IN AMERICAN FOOTBALL: PAST, PRESENT, AND FUTURE

Breaking Barriers and Shaping the Game: Women's Evolving Roles in American Football

Theresa Smith

© Copyright 2024 - All rights reserved.

The content contained within this book may not be reproduced, duplicated or transmitted without direct written permission from the author or the publisher.

Under no circumstances will any blame or legal responsibility be held against the publisher, or author, for any damages, reparation, or monetary loss due to the information contained within this book, either directly or indirectly.

Legal Notice:

This book is copyright protected. It is only for personal use. You cannot amend, distribute, sell, use, quote or paraphrase any part, or the content within this book, without the consent of the author or publisher.

Disclaimer Notice:

Please note the information contained within this document is for educational and entertainment purposes only. All effort has been executed to present accurate, up to date, reliable, complete information. No warranties of any kind are declared or implied. Readers acknowledge that the author is not engaged in the rendering of legal, financial, medical or professional advice. The content within this book has been derived from various sources. Please consult a licensed professional before attempting any techniques outlined in this book.

By reading this document, the reader agrees that under no circumstances is the author responsible for any losses, direct or indirect, that are incurred as a result of the use of the information contained within this document, including, but not limited to, errors, omissions, or inaccuracies.

TABLE OF CONTENTS

—◆—

INTRODUCTION 1

CHAPTER 1: THE EARLY PIONEERS OF WOMEN'S FOOTBALL 5

THE BIRTH OF AMERICAN FOOTBALL AND THE FIRST WOMEN PLAYERS 5
PIONEERING ATTEMPTS AND RESISTANCE TO FEMALE FOOTBALL 8
MOMENTANEOUS THRIVING: THE FORGOTTEN WOMEN'S FOOTBALL LEAGUE OF THE 1930S 12
THE PARADOXICALLY POSITIVE WWII 15

CHAPTER 2: WOMEN'S FOOTBALL DURING WORLD WAR II 17

FOOTBALL DURING WWII IN THE UNITED KINGDOM 17
SPORTS IN THE USA DURING THE WAR 22
SPORTS, FOOTBALL, AND WOMEN IN THE US DURING WWII 26
AMERICAN WOMEN IN WW2 28
POST-WAR 30

CHAPTER 3: THE WOMEN'S FOOTBALL REVIVAL 33

THE WOMEN'S PROFESSIONAL FOOTBALL LEAGUE (1965-1973) 33
FATHER OF AMERICAN WOMEN'S FOOTBALL LEAGUES 35
THE LARGER CULTURAL TREND 38
THE INTERIM LEAGUES 39
THE LEGACY OF THE 20TH CENTURY LEAGUES 41
THE SECOND WOMEN'S PROFESSIONAL FOOTBALL LEAGUE (1999-2007) 42

CHAPTER 4: CURRENT LANDSCAPE OF WOMEN IN AMERICAN FOOTBALL 45

THE WOMEN'S FOOTBALL ALLIANCE AND OTHER CURRENT LEAGUES 45
A PROVOCATIVE IDEA: THE LINGERIE FOOTBALL LEAGUE 48
AN IDEA FOR THE FUTURE 50
JENNIFER WELTER: AN AUTHENTIC PIONEER FOR WOMEN IN AMERICAN FOOTBALL 50
TOUCHDOWNS AND TRIUMPHS: SAM GORDON'S GAME-CHANGING IMPACT ON WOMEN'S FOOTBALL 52
PROMINENT FEMALE FOOTBALL PLAYERS 54
IS FEMINISM INCOMPATIBLE WITH FOOTBALL? 56

CHAPTER 5: BREAKING BARRIERS: WOMEN IN COACHING.......... 59

LORI LOCUST AND MARAL JAVADIFAR: FIRST WOMEN TO WIN THE SUPER BOWL 61
CALLIE BROWNSON: EXCELLENCY INSIDE AND ON THE SIDE OF THE GRIDIRON 65
JENNIFER KING: FIRST BLACK FEMALE NFL COACH 67
KATHRYN SMITH'S JOURNEY TO BECOMING THE NFL'S FIRST FULL-TIME FEMALE COACH 69
KATIE SOWERS: THE FIRST WOMAN TO REACH THE SUPER BOWL 71
COLLEGE COACHING: MINI BOLDEN-MORRIS 72
THE NFL'S COMMITMENT TO DIVERSITY 74

CHAPTER 6: MAKING THEIR VOICES HEARD: WOMEN IN ANNOUNCING 77

THE RISE OF WOMEN IN SPORTS MEDIA 77
BETH MOWINS' PIONEERING CAREER 78
KATE SCOTT'S JOURNALIST JOURNEY 80
TRAILBLAZERS IN SPORTS MEDIA 82
LOOKING TO THE FUTURE 85

CHAPTER 7: BEHIND THE WHISTLE: WOMEN IN REFEREEING 87

PROGRESS AND PERSISTING PROBLEMS 87
HOW TO INCREASE THE REPRESENTATION OF WOMEN IN REFEREEING ROLES 89
OFFICIAL ROBIN DELORENZO 92
MAIA CHAKA: THE FIRST BLACK WOMAN REFEREE IN THE NFL 93
SARAH THOMAS: PUSHING THE LIMITS OF WHAT'S POSSIBLE IN NCAA OFFICIATING 95

CHAPTER 8: FUTURE PROSPECTS FOR WOMEN IN AMERICAN FOOTBALL 99

WOMEN'S SPORTS EVOLUTION 99
EMBRACING TECHNOLOGICAL ADVANCEMENTS TO ENHANCE AMERICAN FOOTBALL'S FUTURE 102
HOW TECHNOLOGY RELATES TO WOMEN'S AMERICAN FOOTBALL 106
"THE GENDER BOWL" 108
THE QUEST FOR EQUALITY IN AMERICAN FOOTBALL 110
THE IMPACT OF ATHLETICS ON FEMALE ACADEMIC ACHIEVEMENT 111
OVERCOMING THE OBSTACLES: INCREASING THE NUMBER OF WOMEN PARTICIPATING IN SPORTS 114
THE INCREASING PARTICIPATION OF WOMEN IN ATHLETICS: A STEP TOWARDS EQUALITY AND EMPOWERMENT 116
UN WOMEN PROMOTES EQUALITY AND WOMEN'S SPORTS 119

CHAPTER 9: IMPACT OF TRAILBLAZING WOMEN ON AMERICAN FOOTBALL 123

MORE WOMEN IN KEY JOBS IN THE NFL 123
WOMEN NFL OWNERS 125

THE NFL'S DRIVE FOR WOMEN'S INCLUSION 129
RESEARCH ON THE UNTOLD JOURNEY OF WOMEN IN AMERICAN FOOTBALL .. 132

CHAPTER 10:   EMPOWERING THE NEXT GENERATION 139

PROVIDING GIRLS WITH THE MEANS TO ACHIEVE SUCCESS AND IMPROVE THEIR
WELL-BEING THROUGH SPORTS 141
LESSONS THAT ARE CRUCIAL FOR GIRLS TO LEARN IN ORDER TO ACHIEVE
SUCCESS IN LIFE 144
THE CONTRIBUTION OF ROLE MODELS AND THE IMPORTANCE OF
ENCOURAGEMENT 146
NAVIGATING THE COMPLEX LANDSCAPE OF YOUTH SPORTS FOR FEMALE
ATHLETES 147
OBSTACLES TO THE PARTICIPATION OF GIRLS AND WOMEN IN
EXTRACURRICULAR ACTIVITIES 150
THE ADDRESSING OF CONCERNS REGARDING HEALTH AND SAFETY IN
WOMEN'S SPORTS 153

CONCLUSION 157

REFERENCES 161

INTRODUCTION

The history of football, or the various versions of football, is extensive and varied and dates back thousands of years. We know that in ancient Greece, two similar team ball games existed: *episkyros* and *faininda*, which resembled modern rugby and American football. Then a Roman version called *harpastum*, played in particular by legionaries in their camps during peace times.

In the Middle Ages, we have a notion about a direct descendant of the Greek and Roman game, played in Italy and in particular Florence, called *calcio*, the name the Italians to this day use for what the Americans call soccer. Florence's *calcio storico*, historical football, is alive even today, with yearly tournaments that gain the interest of many people worldwide. We can also watch some *calcio storico* games of the last years on the Internet. The game's basic setting resembles our modern rugby and American football. The difference is it has an even more violent and raw setting, although with less athleticism and strength, with a mob of amateur players beating each other up more than actually caring about where the ball is.

That's very close to the game played in medieval Great Britain, too, called "mob football." There were no fixed teams and organized leagues, of course, but spontaneous groups, more often made by communities of a town's quarters or villages, which competed and expressed their rivalry in this playful yet not at all peaceful or innocuous way. People played rough and chaotic games across town. Rules and organization were minimal, and the number of individuals who played was large and non-definite in the chaotic setting surrounding the game. Later, we can trace the existence of mob football in France and other European countries, and finally, we can see the beginning of a development that created more organized forms of the game over time.

That development would bring to our modern sports of rugby and American football, as well as a variety of other sports with a common ancestor. They are not secondary sports played only in certain parts of the planet, but some of the most famous and rich sports worldwide, such as soccer, internationally called football, and basketball. Soccer came from rugby in late 19th century England, and physical educator John Naismith, who wanted to find a way to keep his college students at Springfield College in Massachusetts in physical form during winter when practicing outside was impossible, invented basketball in 1891.

The reader could ask, "Fine, so what about women?" We don't know if women participated in that kind of games in Antiquity or the Middle Ages. We can't exclude the possibility that women could have played together with men sometimes or that they formed teams and competitions of their own. Those team ball sports were popular and chaotic, not official, professional, and organized, so why not? Moreover, surprisingly, in the very first mention we have in literature about a ball game, the players are females: It's in Homer's Odyssey, where Nausicaa, the daughter of the king Alcinous of Phaeacia, plays with her friends when suddenly the shipwrecked Odysseus appears.

Can we imagine that women participated in those ball games, the ancient and medieval ancestors of our team sports? Maybe. But one thing is sure: women play every team ball sport we know of in the modern era, and American football is one of them, although not since its beginning. In the following pages, we will see when women first played American football, what held them back, and how, through the decades, they managed to improve their position until women's football was accepted as a sport with its own professional leagues and coverage.

CHAPTER 1:

The Early Pioneers of Women's Football

—◆—

The Birth of American Football and the First Women Players

From its modest origins in casual mob games in medieval Britain and Europe's towns and villages to the systematized and wealthy professional leagues of our time, football's evolution marks changes in the gameplay and broader cultural trends. One of those cultural trends, and especially important for this book, is, of course, the trend toward gender equality.

English public schools in the 19th century had a crucial impact on the game's evolution as they codified norms and regulations. Current regulations came primarily from that initial framework created in that period, during which, in the United States, rugby began evolving into what we know as American football.

Universities of the Ivy League, such as Harvard and Yale, had a central role in shaping American football out of the initial forms of the game. Interestingly, the fact that academic institutions formed the American football rules did not make the game milder in the United States, in contrast to the parallel evolution in Europe. On the contrary, American football maintained a much more violent form of the game compared to British and European rugby. This is not irrelevant to the central theme of this book, gender inclusivity, and, in general, the game's inclusiveness in the US. It's easy to understand that this considerable toughness of American football to this day makes the game more suitable for muscular and more robust persons, i.e., more often men.

The early American tradition of the game includes the so-called "Bloody Monday," which can help us understand American football's origins and nature. "Bloody Monday" was a game played every year between a team of freshmen and a team of sophomores in no less than the University of Harvard, and as the name suggests, it was extremely violent. It was so savage, and there were so many injuries, riots, and clashes following it that in 1860, the university's authorities banned it. Similar was the situation with football in other universities, such as Yale, where the university authorities banned the football game altogether, prohibiting students from playing it on the campus.

After all that, the reader may not be surprised that football in America was substantially exclusive to males in those rough times, and in modern terms, it discriminated against females. Indeed, organized football had an exclusive aspect and did not permit women to play it. There was some progress over time as far as female involvement was concerned, but that discrimination against women interested in playing football went on for many decades, and as we'll see in the next chapter, it was only during the 1960s that women's football leagues came into existence with some consistency.

However, women had been interested in football much earlier. The first documented women's football game occurred in the 19th century, in 1896, although it was not particularly serious. On that occasion, a men's social club had arranged a scrimmage between two female football teams to entertain its male members. It was more like a parody that mocked women instead of including them in the football realm, one could say today. Yet, it was an all-women football game, which proves that there were women who wanted to play already at that time and men who were willing to watch them, even as a joke.

Gaining respectability was not an easy job for women's football throughout the following century; on the contrary, they faced strong opposition from many directions in participating and playing the game of football. There were far worse things, of course. One of the factors that diminished women's engagement in football was the very fact that they were not allowed to study at universities. We talked about Harvard and Yale's banning football in the early 1860s. Even when they accepted the game back in more organized forms, and their football teams were thriving in the early 20th century, together with other institutions such as Princeton, they did not include female students. The latter were allowed to study in exclusively women's institutions, such as the Radcliffe College in Cambridge, Massachusetts, founded in 1879.

By the early 1920s, female students played football in universities such as Minnesota's Gustavus Adolphus; however, female students and players could not play in organized college football leagues. The lack of interest and the lack of support and assistance from the most important and established institutions on the football field kept women's football on the sidelines, without the resources to grow into something more meaningful in American sports.

Pioneering Attempts and Resistance to Female Football

The first attempts to establish women's football leagues were short-lived, and women's participation in football would remain marginal for many years. Yet, if one examines them, the initial glimpses we've just talked about are much more interesting than they might appear at first sight, keeping in mind the broader sociological changes and evolution of that time.

Indeed, in the early 20th century, and especially during the 1920s, a new chapter in sports history was opened in parallel with broader societal transformations and evolution. As the industrial era progressed and grew, changing the objective conditions of human life in the most advanced countries, gender boundaries gradually blurred and then were challenged and reinterpreted. The decisive, pioneering women who took to the gridiron, ignoring societal norms contrary to women's participation in football, were an example of that broader trend, as they disregarded stereotypes and paved the way for future generations.

In that decade, there were indeed several cases where women played tackle football, demonstrating that they were much more agile and resilient than previously believed. The pioneering women players performed on a series of occasions, from exhibition games at Gustavus Adolphus, which we have already mentioned, to the halftime show of games of the Frankford Yellow Jackets, who played in the National Football League, the first professional American football league.

One of those events occurred in 1926 at Cavour High School in South Dakota. It is most often ignored in the history of women's football, but it is really pioneering and inspiring. Some female students, knowing that the number of boys who played football and formed the high school's team was not so high, decided to create two teams of their own. They called the teams Alphas and Betas and insisted on playing football, although the school's authorities were against this practice of theirs. The girls' initiative and determination created enthusiasm in the local community, which supported them and made their town famous for a while. We can imagine the inspiring impact news like that could have had locally and in various other places, thanks to those girls' unyielding spirit and their love for the game.

However, despite those pioneering women's determination and dedication and the attention they received nationwide, standards of society and sexist attitudes continued to resist the development of women's football. There were concerns and medical professionals' opinions and warnings according to which women were physically fragile and at risk of being badly injured if they played competitive full-contact football. It's evident that this kind of language underestimated and lowered the abilities and talent of women players, making them appear inferior and not suitable for football.

Fortunately, other sports were more socially acceptable for female athletes to play, such as softball, which was the sport the Marshall-Clampett Amazons mostly embraced and practiced in those years, among many other female athletes. Softball offered opportunities women didn't have in other sports and, most of all, in American football. Some of those female athletes also appeared in Hollywood films next to cinema stars of that era or made tours in various places worldwide.

On the other hand, and as good and profitable as opportunities of that kind could be for female athletes individually, they continued to portray female athletes as a category not entirely dedicated to practicing competitive sports but using sports to obtain access to more acceptable roles for women, such as playing in movies. The notion that physically demanding sports were incompatible with femininity persisted for an extended period in modern history, causing continuous and persistent objections and contrast to sportswomen's attempts to achieve equal treatment on the playing field.

The Marshall-Clampett Amazons' achievements are one example of sportswomen who defied preconceptions and overcame boundaries, along with other cases such as Senda Berenson's resilient work in establishing women's basketball. Similar cases paved the way and empowered future generations of female athletes to claim and secure a better and more equal position for women's sports in society.

For its part, the sport we focus on in this book, American football, has always been the most difficult case in history when it comes to accepting women players, and it continues to be so. The women who had the courage to walk on the field despite old cultural conventions and prejudice faced only more discrimination and resistance against their choice to play football and not a proper "feminine" sport as, according to a part of society, they should have done.

Many of those women played sporadically in places such as Los Angeles and Bethlehem, Pennsylvania, but the authorities treated them in a way that seems incredible and incomprehensible to us now. The parks, which until then had allowed women to play football on their grounds, suddenly prohibited all such women's football games, excluding them in a severe and discriminatory manner.

The reason and the driving force behind that attitude, which seems crazy to us now, was a view that again may seem at least extremely exaggerated, if not lunatic. Many officials had a deep worry that allowing women to play a supposedly ultra-masculine game, such as football, would put at risk society's fabric itself, subverting the ideals of femininity and its role. Football was seen as the "most masculine activity imaginable," so a significant part of the establishment saw the possibility of women playing and participating in this game as unacceptable and socially dangerous. They even prompted measures and restrictions against opposing opinions.

The case of the administrator of the parks department in Bethlehem is striking. He said clearly and openly that women playing football could herald a new era where gender roles would be dissolved and the boundaries between them lost. That would be a disaster, and on the contrary, women should maintain what he understood as a feminine nature, symbolized by the "typical American girl:" a perfectly feminine female who bled elegance and charm and naturally had no masculine traits and tendencies.

There were also favorable forces to the emergence of women's sports outside the deep-rooted hostility and repression against women's football. In 1941, a professional women's basketball league was created, with teams such as the Chicago Rockets and the New York Bombers; yet, it had no success as it couldn't raise an audience. People did not find a league formed by women's basketball teams interesting, and the attempt only met apathy and disinterest. Of course, despite the fact the dominant culture was, as we saw, indifferent or contrary to women's sports, one should add that those were the years of WWII. Even men's basketball was far from what it came to be in later decades in terms of spectators and popularity.

Momentaneous Thriving: The Forgotten Women's Football League of the 1930s

Between the two World Wars, women's football was a unique phenomenon that momentarily captivated the attention of sports fans nationwide. However, this innovative trend lasted only for one season. After the end of its inaugural season, it vanished into oblivion despite having a promising beginning and significant media coverage. What was left behind was unresolved issues and untold stories.

The most important primary sources for that brief trend are photographs from publications that had a large audience, like "Life" and "Click." In these pictures one can see women confident and ready to take on the difficulties of the gridiron field, dressed in complete football uniforms. However, apart from the photos, there is not much information in the magazines about who those trailblazer women were and what their aspirations were.

With a touch of imagination, one can see those images and stories coming out of the shadows of American sports history, telling us that there is a long-forgotten tale of women's football we mostly don't know anything about. Yet, it is a fascinating story of ambition, courage, and the search for athletic recognition, which challenged the societal rules of that time. The establishment of a women's football league in the 1930s was an authentic pioneering adventure, which had the courage and audacity to confront gender limitations and prejudices that existed back then in sports and in broader society.

It is odd that most of the football players who formed the backbone of the women's football league in the 1930s were previously softball players known for their physical skills. This one-of-a-kind metamorphosis took place in Los Angeles while women's softball was at the peak of its popularity. The Marshall-Clampett Amazons were the squad that spearheaded this change from one sport to another. They were a team that not only did well in softball but also ventured into football, proving their adaptability and shattering the gender stereotypes that were pervasive in their day. Moreover, by the end of the interim period between the two world wars, women's football would have a moment of celebrity nationwide in 1939, when the Marshall-Clampett Amazons played against the Chet Relph Hollywood Stars in Los Angeles, and publications such as Life Magazine and the Los Angeles Times covered the event. It was the first full-contact public women's American football game, that is, not an exhibition game but a real competition, which shattered prejudices against the capacity of women to play real competitive football.

So, at least in part, the founding of the women's football league's founding was a clever and innovative attempt to profit from softball's popularity. The plan was for the football league to prolong the season and the sports spectacle during the months after the softball season conclusion, filling the vacuum with football from autumn to winter. The growing interest in women's sports in that period becomes evident if we think that there were audiences of more than 3,000 people and that the initiative gained the strong interest of the press.

The league was met with criticism and worries over the safety of women playing football, a sport that has historically been associated with masculinity and brutality. Despite the excitement, the league received scrutiny and criticism. Concerns of this kind, in conjunction with the players' stable dedication to the sport of softball, in the end, resulted in the collapse of the league. When compared to the potential of a growing football league that was having difficulty expanding, the allure of softball, with its chances for film appearances and foreign tours, was more appealing.

The league had difficulties, although it drew over 3,000 spectators and attracted national media attention. Some had negative responses to the games, seeing them as a challenge to masculinity. Others expressed worries about safety, which echoed current discussions about women playing contact sports. Historian Michael Oriard hypothesizes that societal norms of the day that connected football to masculinity may have contributed to the league's demise. Still, the players' preexisting commitments to softball—which provided more possibilities and incentives than football—were the main cause of the league's downfall. For a softball player in 1930s Los Angeles, the prestige of playing abroad, film appearances, and travel abroad was more appealing than the short-lived reputation of women's football.

In the summer of 1941, an effort was made to organize a second league in Chicago, which brought about a new chapter in the history of women's football. However, much like its predecessor, this project could only last for a short period of time. The interest was very small, and eventually, the project failed and went out of business. World War II created new needs, and the allocation of resources changed, as did the interest of the public.

Nevertheless, the attempts made in the 1930s to create women's football leagues are a notable story in the history of women's sports in the United States. The leagues had short lives and did not consolidate in the reality of American sports, but they manifested the female athletes' aim to overcome restricting traditional gender norms and take part in competitive sports on their own terms. Those old attempts ultimately did not succeed, but the experiences of those female football players contributed greatly to creating the necessary narrative and preparing the way.

In the 1970s, women's football saw a comeback, which coincided with the establishment of a semi-professional league. This occurred at a time when there was a revived interest in the sport despite the fact that it also encountered difficulties in achieving general recognition. The history of these early women's football leagues serves as a reminder of the relentless attempts that have been made to break down boundaries and alter the landscape of American sports. This is especially relevant in light of the ongoing conversations that are taking place around gender equality in sports.

The tale of the Marshall-Clampett Amazons and their equivalents serves as a moving reminder of the intricate relationship between gender, athletics, and entertainment at a time when worries about football safety, in general, are only growing. There is still no guarantee that a professional women's football league will manage to consolidate. Women's football leagues came and went in the 1930s, but their legacy lives on as a tribute to the pioneering nature of female players and the difficulties they overcame to follow their love of the game. As we consider their path, we are reminded of the continuous struggle for opportunity and equality in the sports industry.

The Paradoxically Positive WWII

The war paradoxically worked wonders for women's football, though. With many young men joining the army and the various fronts, there came to be a scarcity of football players back home, and that offered a window of opportunity for female players to step up. The ones to try it first were the female students at Eastern State University, who entered the field wearing the university team's jerseys and played very well. The girls delighted and impressed the spectators by performing with great passion and being highly energetic.

However, women's football's momentous flourishing was about to fade away very soon. After the war, everything returned to normal, with women's football in the background.

As a heartbreaking reminder of the ongoing fight for gender equality and acknowledgment in the world of sports, the tale of the first attempts to establish and make women's football socially acceptable serves as a powerful example of this fight. Those women had the guts to defy expectations and challenge societal norms, paving the way for future generations of female athletes. They accomplished this despite the fact that they often encountered tremendous obstacles and persistent prejudice in their communities.

In the next chapter, we'll discuss the WWII period and the growth of women's football in those dramatic conditions. We will begin with a sight abroad and international side of football before returning to the United States.

CHAPTER 2:

Women's Football During World War II

—◆—

Football During WWII in the United Kingdom

During the turbulent years of World War II, the English Football Association (FA) played a significant part in keeping the spirit of the country alive via the game of football. This was accomplished despite the destruction that occurred and the critical need for activities that would raise morale.

Following the outbreak of the war, the football season was immediately put on hold, and young Englishmen, even those who were playing professionally, were forced to serve in the military. This decision, which was made in order to comply with a restriction on mass gatherings, was greeted with significant unhappiness among supporters, which revealed the profound significance of football in British culture as well as the deep-seated enthusiasm that fans have for the sport.

The Football Association came up with a brilliant solution to this problem by establishing seven regional leagues that provided competition without placing any undue pressure on the nation's transportation infrastructure, which was essential for the war effort. In order to reduce the likelihood of German bombing attacks, the number of people who could attend games was initially limited to 8,000. Conversely, this ban was gradually relaxed as the immediate threat posed by explosives throughout the day decreased. This was done in acknowledgment of football's ability to raise public spirits and maintain a feeling of normalcy in the face of such difficult circumstances. Football stadiums, which were often located near urban areas or next to industrial areas, were also inadvertent targets of aircraft bombs during this time period. Manchester United and Arsenal were compelled to move their home games because of the significant damage that was done to famous venues like Highbury and Old Trafford.

The tenacity of the football community shined brightly in spite of these problems, as shown by the fact that teams occasionally had to ask supporters to fill in places in order to complete an 11-man roster owing to a scarcity of players. Several British football players heroically served heroically on the front lines throughout the war, but they, too, had to make sacrifices. Harry Goslin, the captain of Bolton Wanderers, and his colleagues showed this sacrifice. The one who would ultimately perish in Italy was Goslin, in particular. The war had a significant influence on football since it had an effect on every team and left behind a legacy of courage and resiliency.

During World War II, Stanley Matthews, a legendary figure in the sport, participated in the Royal Air Force, demonstrating the participation of highly accomplished sportsmen in the war effort. Matthews's commitment to football and his nation is unquestionable, as proven by the fact that he was knighted and inducted into the English Football Hall of Fame. This is despite the fact that his image has been tarnished only somewhat by his involvement in activities related to the black market.

Not only did this period of wartime football, which was characterized by adaptation and bravery, serve as an essential distraction for the general population, but it also highlighted the significant position that football plays in the culture and society of the United Kingdom. The players' determination to give up in the face of adversity in order to serve their country and the game is a testament to the perseverance of the football spirit.

Ladies' Football During WWII in the UK

Despite many obstacles and limitations, women athletes' tenacity and will were evident on the field during the tumult of World War II in the United Kingdom.

British women's football, or soccer as the Americans call it, originated in the Great War, i.e., World War I, when teams made up of munitions workers popularized the game. Following WWI, women's football spread across the nation. The sport had grown to new heights by June 1939, near the beginning of WWII, when elite teams were vying for the Championship in Scotland. Among the competitors were the Rutherglen Ladies, the 1923 champions, but it was former Rutherglen player Linda Clements who took center stage. As a player for the Edinburgh City Girls, Clements's two goals helped her side win handily over Preston Ladies. Her team then went on to dominate Glasgow Ladies to win the championship.

Those beautiful romantic images of women's sports summer noons and crowds cheering would shortly meet the dark and brutal reality of World War II erupted on September 1, 1939, quickly putting a dampener on the developing football and, in general, sports scene. Nevertheless, women's football matches continued in Britain in the early going of the conflict, which was nicknamed the "phony war," particularly between the Preston Ladies and the recently established Bolton Ladies. However, several teams encountered difficulties as the conflict became more intense. The Rutherglen Ladies and Preston Ladies stopped competing in favor of focusing their energies on generating money for the war effort via charity events and other projects.

Even with these obstacles, women's football made progress. Factory football teams evolved as more women entered the labor force in munitions factories and other support sectors, demonstrating a spirit of resilience and camaraderie. Funds were raised for local organizations and military charities by organizing matches between teams made of industrial workers and support personnel and even between teams of married against single women.

Amidst the war, the county of Kent in South-East England established its own women's football league in 1944, disregarding directives from the national football authorities. The Aylsham Ladies, a group of female players from the Snowdown Colliery, won the title and showed that despite hardship, they could still have a strong love for the game.

The trip wasn't without its challenges, however. The Football Association had placed severe limitations on women's football since 1921 and had not lifted them, not even during wartime. Moreover, big stadiums continued to be unavailable, depriving women of the chance to perform on a vast scale.

Despite these difficulties, women's football during World War II is an example of players' tenacity, willpower, and stubborn spirit. Women continued to play, energizing communities and challenging social conventions in everything from munitions workers' teams to industrial matches. In spite of all obstacles, they kept the football flame burning bright during one of humanity's worst moments. Their legacy lives on, serving as a source of inspiration and hope for the next generations of female athletes.

In addition to being a tale of fortitude on the field in difficult times, the history of women's football during WWII also reveals the divergent viewpoints of the organizations in charge of the sport. Although women in the UK were uniting on the field and confronting obstacles head-on, the Football Association (FA) and the Scottish Football Association (SFA) continued to show resistance and even animosity toward the emerging women's game.

The FA's position in England throughout the war years was unwavering. There are several examples of the association interfering with and opposing women's matches. An FA intervention resulted in the sudden cancellation of a football match organized by the Women's Land Army at London Road, Peterborough United, in 1943. Furthermore, Mr. H. R. Rigdem was sacked from his long-standing role as Rochester league secretary by the Kent County FA for his involvement as an official in a women's match played at Medway Town.

Nevertheless, things were noticeably different in Scotland. Although the SFA was not so favorable, the attitude toward women's football was, in many cases, noticeably different in comparison with England. Women's football was accepted in certain quarters. Prominent individuals like the players on the Rangers team, Jerry Dawson and Alex Venters, refereed women's football games, demonstrating a more accepting mindset toward women in the sport; also, famed Scotland international player George Young officiated a women's match between Barr & Stroud and Switchgear in Kirkintilloch.

Auxiliary forces emerged throughout the war effort, with women enlisting in newly established corps like the Auxiliary Territorial Services and the Women's Auxiliary Air Force. Football players often get professional instruction, and the sport has grown to be an essential component of the military leisure program. As matches between service teams and labor teams increased in frequency, women's football continued to flourish despite the difficulties of war.

The post-war boom in women's football occurred after hostilities ended. Demobilized military women were welcomed into the ranks of newly created and reestablished teams, which helped to spark a revival of the game. Still, the official response remained ambiguous. In a newspaper interview, senior Edinburgh football personality Linda Clements pointed out the SFA's conflicted feelings over women's football. Despite their increasing popularity, women's matches were not recognized by the SFA, which made it difficult to get performance permits. The SFA remained opposed in the next years, mirroring the FA's attitude in England. Nevertheless, women's football continued, finding patrons in unorthodox settings like workplaces and factories. Despite having a major influence on the expansion and development of women's football, the years from 1939 to 1945 are still not well-researched in the history of the sport.

Sports in the USA During the War

In the United States, the dynamic spirit of athletics persisted during the turmoil of World War II, and furthermore, it served as a beacon of morale and solidarity. The world of sports created a place of normality and happiness in the middle of those turbulent years that were marked by violence and rationing.

Boxing was a prominent force in American sports throughout the 1930s and 1940s. People like Joe Louis were able to draw crowds and popularize boxing because of their achievements in the ring, which served as a symbol of strength and hope. The victory that Louis achieved against Max Schmeling in 1938 transcended the realm of sports and became a moving story of perseverance against the background of world tensions. In contrast to Louis, who would go on to serve in the United States Army and provide boxing performances to the soldiers in order to cheer them up, Schmeling would go on to join the German paratroopers, signaling a different route that was anchored in the same sport.

A lengthy shadow was thrown over American athletics by the onset of World War II, which resulted in substantial modifications and alterations throughout that time period. It is noteworthy that the All-American Girls Baseball League was established in 1943; this is a demonstration of the flexibility and lasting spirit that exists within the world of sports. The league was established by William K. Wrigley, and it included teams such as the Rockford Peaches and the Kalamazoo Lassies. Its purpose was to highlight the remarkable abilities and dogged resolve of female athletes at a period in which many men were serving in the military. Not only did this league, which combined aspects of baseball and softball, fill stadiums, but it also served as a source of inspiration for subsequent generations, and it was finally memorialized in the film A League of Their Own.

Baseball, a sport that had already established itself in Japan decades before, did not see much of a decline in popularity as a result of the war. Japanese professional players who were asked to serve their nation proved that the game has a worldwide reach and that its value transcends cultural barriers. During this time period, the global attraction of athletics as a source of identity and pride was brought to light, even in the midst of the challenges that war presented.

The war had a significant influence on American football, with collegiate football witnessing a boom in popularity over its professional counterpart. This was due to the fact that the war was taking place. In the course of the draft, hundreds of college athletes chose to wear military uniforms rather than the colors of their teams, a movement that had a significant impact on the collegiate athlete. As a demonstration of the war's pervasive influence on every aspect of American life, football activities were halted at a variety of educational institutions around the country, including Harvard and Stanford.

Even in the face of these obstacles, the fundamental characteristics of sports, which include perseverance, unity, and the unrelenting quest for perfection, shone brilliantly. It is a reflection of the connected storylines of sports and service that figures such as Tom Landry, who would go on to become a great coach for the Dallas Cowboys, sacrificed themselves for their country. Heroic deeds performed by athletes such as Maurice Britt and Jack Lummus, who were awarded the Medal of Honor, are illustrative of the great bravery and self-sacrifice shown by individuals who turned their attention away from the athletic arena and onto the battlefield.

While World War II was changing the face of the planet, it was also redefining the sports world and demonstrating the ability of athletics to inspire, unite, and heal. The time proved that sportsmen have an unwavering drive to succeed and that sports will always inspire and unite people, even amid the most trying situations. This was seen everywhere, from the boxing ring to the baseball fields.

The world of sports went through a period of terrible loss and great bravery in the shadow of the worldwide struggle that was World War II. This transcended the borders between countries and the battlegrounds of both sport and combat. During this time period, the sacrifices made by athletes who left the playing fields and arenas to serve on the front lines were brought to light. These athletes exemplified the spirit of perseverance and solidarity.

On the beaches of Iwo Jima, Jack Lummus, who would later become a Marine Corps officer and a player for the New York Giants in the National Football League, exemplified the ultimate sacrifice. It is a monument to the tenacious spirit that is shared by sportsmen and warriors alike that Lummus led his troops with unwavering bravery until his dying moments, despite the fact that he had suffered grievous injuries.

In a similar manner, Jack Chevigny and Howard "Smiley" Johnson, both of whom were college football stars before the war, met their deaths on Iwo Jima, which exemplifies the extensive influence that the war had on the world of sports. Their stories, along with those of others, shed light on the harsh reality that athletes who showed distinction and heroism while serving their country experienced.

Athletes from Canada were heavily impacted by the war's toll, which went beyond the borders of the United States.

The National Hockey League persisted in spite of the call to arms, which resulted in the deaths of a great number of players, notably Dudley "Red" Garrett and Joe Turner, who were volunteering for military duty. Rugby and a variant of American football, two of Canada's most treasured sports, were also susceptible to the effects of the war, with leagues stopping play as a result of the conscription of a significant number of players. Jevon "Jeff" Nicklin, a top player for the Winnipeg Blue Bombers and a member of the Royal Canadian Air Force Hurricanes football team, who won the Grey Cup in 1942, typified the tremendous losses that Canadian sports have had to face. Through their sacrifices, they raised awareness of the prevailing mindset in the sports world: a collective desire to promote the greater good.

The National Basketball League was in charge of providing a sizable number of players to the armed forces throughout the conflict, which was also a significant time for the game of basketball. Athletes such as Bob "Ace" Calkins and Edward C. Christi exemplified the breadth of the war's influence with their participation in a variety of sports and their ability to touch the lives of countless others via their tales of courage and sacrifice. A devastating reminder of the human cost of battle and the unyielding spirit of those who strive for success, whether on the field or in the theater of war, these accounts from the world of sports during World War II give a painful reminder of both of these things.

Sports, Football, and Women in the US During WWII

During World War II, sports were not only important for the men and women serving in the armed forces but also had a big impact on the civilian population, reflecting and enhancing the nation's prevailing patriotic spirit. In order to cultivate a sports culture that is known to troops from their civilian lives, the military extended its athletic program, which had been founded during World War I. This was accomplished by supplying equipment, training, and staff. The public relations of the Department of War were improved as a result of the participation of a large number of well-known sportsmen in military duty. This helped to build the connection between sports and patriotism.

President Franklin D. Roosevelt declared that sports would continue normally despite the war due to the advantages they provide in terms of raising morale. This brought to light the relevance of sports in preserving national spirit and identity. Through the celebration of military achievement in sports, the United States of America was able to further strengthen its reputation as a strong and resilient country.

That regarded, first of all, baseball. An inquiry made by Commissioner Kenesaw "Mountain" Landis to President Roosevelt on the continuation of baseball during the war resulted in the famous "green light letter," which backed the significance of maintaining baseball as a means of boosting national morale. The resilience and tenacity of the American people was shown by Major League Baseball's prolonged existence in spite of the war's consequences and the fact that many of its most well-known players were enlisting in the military.

American football had then a special treatment, as it was considered the most masculine sport, and that, of course, was lined up with what the American military needed and conveyed at that time. Some of the most important generals of WWII, such as Dwight Eisenhower, Douglas MacArthur, George Marshall, and Omar Bradley, openly advocated for American football as an excellent game and also for the training of the troops in the camps, as the Roman legionaries did with their own similar game back in ancient times, as we've seen in the introduction of this book. Football was generally held in high esteem by those in positions of authority inside the military. During the war years, the Army and Navy football teams were the dominant force in college football. Armed Forces Radio was used to transmit their games to soldiers all over the globe while they were playing. There was a temporary reduction in the size of the NFL as a result of a considerable proportion of its players being involved in the war effort.

That fact impacted women's sports, too, and became much more central in civil life in the country. The need for more workers and soldiers because of the massive participation of men in the war prompted, for the first time, women to leave their homes and their domestic occupations and join occupations traditionally related almost exclusively to men. Women participated in a wide range of sports as they joined the labor force and the military in unprecedented numbers. These activities ranged from basketball and softball in industrial leagues to tennis, golf, and skiing in more wealthy circles. There was a significant amount of progress achieved by black female competitors in the sport of track and field, which laid the foundation for their subsequent supremacy in Olympic contests. Of course, that trend was far from canceling sexist conceptions and overcoming the limits that still existed in women's sports. But it was a good start, like in many other fields.

Because of this, World War II was a time of significant transformation and adaptation for American athletics. This was a reflection of greater cultural transformations as well as the nation's united will to succeed in the face of global strife.

American Women in WW2

As we saw in the previous section, WWII and the lack of men from various posts it brought with it due to their participation in the army prompted women to work in fields that, before the war, were almost exclusively covered by men. Women were encouraged to enter the workforce via campaigns like the well-known Rosie the Riveter campaign. American women revolutionized the workforce and society during World War II by playing crucial roles in the armed forces and at home. During this time, women's roles and cultural expectations underwent a dramatic shift that dispelled preconceptions and increased the extent of their contributions to the economy and war effort.

World War II brought enormous disaster to the world but was also the turning point for many changes in societies. One of them was the substantial shift in the American workforce. Before the war, women's employment was largely confined to specific sectors, and for the rest, their role was to stay at home and take care of domestic matters upon marriage or childbirth. However, since males were enlisting in the army in large numbers during the war, there was a shortage of labor in many industries and factories, which resulted in the entry of nearly five million women into the workforce between 1940 and 1945. Women started to join areas that had historically been controlled by males. One such business was the aviation industry, where, by 1943, women made up the majority in several facilities.

That doesn't mean women did not continue to face numerous challenges, like wage disparities, aversion from parts of society for their occupation as workers, and the objective difficulties in balancing work outside the home with familial responsibilities. On the other hand, the government tried to respond to some of those challenges, and the Community Facilities Act of 1942 established facilities to support mothers working outside the house. The creation of many childcare facilities was a product of that objective need created by the necessity of women joining the labor force.

Military service opened another significant professional path for women during World War II, with approximately 350,000 women serving in various capacities of the armed forces.

Women worked as administrative assistants, mechanics, pilot trainees, and nurses. The United States faced fresh difficulties after the war, as we'll see in the following section. In addition to being urged to take on more home responsibilities, many women lost their employment from the war. However, the earlier tendency had paid off, and the new circumstances were largely permanent as more cultural changes brought about by the expansion of the economy started to take place. Thus, a considerable percentage of women, especially married women, were still employed in 1950 despite advertisements encouraging them to return to domestic jobs, highlighting the long-lasting effects of World War II on women's employment and social responsibilities.

Post-War

We've already seen that during World War II, women filled tasks typically filled by men and joined the workforce in unprecedented numbers. They had greater freedoms and opportunities while working in factories, offices, and other support positions for the war effort instead of staying at home. But a profound change happened when men returned from serving in the armed forces. Women had to return for their part to becoming housewives after leaving the workforce in large numbers, both willingly and reluctantly.

Peace brought an initial comeback of traditional family values, particularly the notion that women's occupation was primarily to take care of domestic work. Birthrates and marriage rates also skyrocketed, indicating a return to pre-war standards in society.

Nevertheless, the shift that had been made could not be entirely forgotten. Women who had worked and been active outside their houses did not forget their experiences during the war and this new way of life, which introduced a sense of independence instead of being tied to pre-established stereotypical roles. The war had given women hope that they might succeed outside the house and defy older social expectations. Prominent personalities championed gender equality, including first lady Eleanor Roosevelt and civil rights activist and later Reverend Pauli Murray. Their words struck a chord with women all throughout the nation, motivating a generation to challenge gender norms and fight for more rights and opportunities.

The war had equipped American women to question the established status quo and lay the groundwork for subsequent decades. Although many women returned to domesticity in the post-war period, it also laid the groundwork for the feminist movements of the 1960s and beyond. Women's contributions and sacrifices during World War II were remembered, and in the years that followed, they acted as a spark for advancement and societal change.

Although there was unquestionably a return to conventional household values, the complicated interaction of governmental regulations, cultural expectations, and the long-lasting effects of wartime experiences led to a permanent change in women's roles in mid-20th century America after the war that continues to define our time.

CHAPTER 3:

The Women's Football Revival

—◆—

The Women's Professional Football League (1965-1973)

There are pioneering and groundbreaking initiatives that can often be disregarded in history, and especially in American sports history. The Women's Professional Football League (WPFL), which was founded by talent agent Sid Friedman in 1965 and stayed in business until 1973, is definitely one of them. This innovative project was the first attempt to establish an organized women's professional football league, and although it could not consolidate its presence in the American sports industry, it opened the way for other similar endeavors. It's not an overstatement to say that the WPFL was the entrance into a new era of possibility in sports, as after the WPFL, a series of women's football leagues were created in the following decades, including the ones existing right now.

The four teams that were established for the first WPFL season were the Detroit Petticoats, the Cleveland Daredevils, the Toronto Canadian Belles, and the Pittsburgh All-Stars (later renamed the Hurricanes and subsequently the Powderkegs). These teams' players were trailblazers who didn't hesitate to go against the grain and follow their love of the game of football. The talent and determination that typified the WPFL were shown by Marcella Sanborn of the Cleveland Daredevils, one of the league's most exceptional players.

The WPFL brought women's football to a wider public by making appearances at halftime displays during games of NFL and CFL teams; it also gave a primary emphasis on exhibition and charity games. The league persisted in spite of obstacles and limited resources, growing in stature and impact by 1971 when it had 15 teams.

That growth of the WPFL led the league to the decision to create an East Division and a West Division, with clubs located in cities ranging from Buffalo and New York to Los Angeles and Portland. The emergence of new teams demonstrated how women's football was becoming more and more popular and accepted as more players seized the chance to play professionally.

Unfortunately, it wasn't meant to last for long, though. By 1973, all the teams disbanded except for the Toledo Troopers of Toledo, Ohio, which joined the recently established National Women's Football League (NWFL). The project proved to be unsustainable, yet the foundation of a second league right before the dissolution of the WPFL proved that the seed that had been planted was already bearing fruit.

Even though it was only around for a short while, the WPFL had a significant impact and helped to inspire later generations of female athletes. Its influence extended beyond the football field, motivating women all throughout the nation to follow their athletic goals and dispel gender preconceptions in the sports industry.

When we consider the history of women's football, we should not overlook the WPFL pioneers, whose bravery and tenacity cleared the way for the amazing advancements and successes that we see in women's sports to this day. Even if their league may no longer exist, their efforts live on as a tribute to the strength of willpower, ardor, and the game's eternal spirit.

Father of American Women's Football Leagues

Sid Friedman appears as a lesser-known yet key character in the women's variation of the sport of American football. If Walter Camp is acclaimed as the Father of American Football for his crucial role in designing the game, then Sid Friedman emerges as a similar figure in the women's version of the sport. Friedman was an enterprising promoter from Cleveland who had a great eye for spectacle above sport. He carved out a place for himself in the 1960s.

Friedman's decision to get into the women's football league was motivated more by business interests than by equitable concerns. Whether it was ladies playing football or pups for a possible "Puppy Bowl," he was interested in the sport. His attitude to the sport was crystal clear: he was interested in the activity if there was an audience and the possibility of profit. Friedman unwittingly built the foundation for the National Women's Football League (NWFL), a pioneering platform that, from 1974 to 1988, made it possible for women all throughout North America to participate in professional football. This was accomplished despite the fact that Friedman was more concerned with maximizing financial gain than promoting actual sports competition.

The NWFL provided a chance for a wide variety of women to participate in the sport. These women included housewives as well as students, and they were able to break away from the traditional roles that were expected of them if they participated in the sport. Marion Motley, a former running back for the Cleveland Browns and a member of the National Football League Hall of Fame, took over as head coach of Friedman's squad despite the fact that there were institutional hurdles against Black coaches in men's football. This was a significant step forward for the league in terms of its commitment to diversity.

Nevertheless, the path of women's football and the themes of struggle, commercial exploitation, and resilience that it has uncovered shed light on a more comprehensive discussion about gender, sport, and visibility. Friedman's inaugural league, which was defined by its pursuit of publicity and gimmicks, such as the proposed usage of tearaway skirts, highlights the commercialization and sexualization of female athletes that have been prevalent in sports for a long time. However, the purpose of this method was not to recognize the physical abilities of women on the field; rather, it was to amuse male spectators.

An example of this fight is provided by Gail Dearie, who was a player for the New York Fillies. The shift that she made from being a model to a wide receiver in football was sensationalized by the media, which focused more on her attractiveness and the fact that she deviated from the typical gender roles than on her overall athletic abilities. These kinds of tales shed light on the persistent difficulty of accomplishing the goal of providing female athletes with equal attention and support.

In spite of the many developments and increased prominence that women's football leagues have brought forth, the legacy of these leagues continues to be bittersweet. Iterations of the Lingerie League, which was eventually renamed the Legends Football League, are examples of how the sexualization of female athletes continues to take place. When compared to their male counterparts, women's sports continue to face persistent discrepancies in funding and infrastructure. These disparities are highlighted by difficulties such as insufficient equipment and a lack of medical insurance coverage.

A key set of concerns about the role of gender in sports and the social assessment of women's athletic activities are brought up when one considers the history and development of women's football. The struggle for actual equality, recognition, and respect within the sport of football continues despite the fact that Friedman's league and its successors have blazed the way for women in football. The tale of women's football is not just about triumphing against opponents on the field; it is also about fighting and reforming the cultural and social conventions that have, for a long time, marginalized their contributions and accomplishments in the world of sports.

The late 20th century saw the emergence of women's football leagues, which represented a major but underrecognized transition in the landscape of American football. This transformation was characterized by the introduction of women's football leagues. Sid Friedman, an entrepreneur whose foresight and confidence gave rise to the first semblance of a professional league for women, was a pivotal figure in this development. The United States of America Daredevils, Friedman's first endeavor, established that women's football had the capacity to attract large audiences and play aggressively, even against teams that are comprised of males. Consequently, this paved the way for the establishment of a number of teams, one of which being the well-known Toledo Troopers, which marked the beginning of a new era in the sport.

The Larger Cultural Trend

On the other hand, Friedman was not the only one responsible for the adventure. Women's football came into being at the same time as a larger cultural change toward gender equality, which posed a challenge to the conventional roles and expectations that had been in place. In spite of the fact that players did not necessarily consider themselves to be feminists, their involvement in the sport was obviously a statement against the standards that were prevalent throughout their respective eras. They were motivated by a variety of causes, including a passion for the game, a need for community, and a quest for personal accomplishment, regardless of the cultural markers that they were associated with.

The history of women's football is filled with tales of tenacity, solidarity, and resistance against the established order all throughout the sport's history. Players such as Linda Jefferson and teams like the Los Angeles Dandelions and the Toledo Troopers not only displayed amazing athleticism but also expanded the limits of what women might strive to be in the world of sports. For example, Jefferson's great skill on the field, which surpassed the traditional physical stereotypes connected with football, led to her becoming a sports legend. She was lauded for her amazing talent.

In addition to further institutionalizing women's involvement in football, Bob Mathews' establishment of the National Women's Football League (NWFL) was essential in spreading the league's reach throughout the United States and establishing the groundwork for the acknowledgment of women's contributions to the sport. In spite of the fact that the league was eventually disbanded, the fact that it existed pushed against the obstacles that prevented women from fully participating in football and brought attention to the need to provide more assistance and recognition to female players.

On the other hand, the fight for equality in athletics is still ongoing. The narrative of the NWFL sheds light on the ongoing obstacles that female athletes must overcome in order to achieve parity with their male counterparts. These obstacles range from concerns over ownership and representation to difficulties with media depiction and public support. Future generations may draw inspiration and motivation from the pioneers of women's football's history as the sport develops to strive toward attaining equity in all facets of sports.

A microcosm of the larger struggle for gender equality in sports is shown in the development of women's football from Friedman's spectacle to a league that is acknowledged. This serves as a reminder of the continual path towards creating a fair playing field in all facets of sports and society, as well as a monument to the resiliency of female athletes.

The Interim Leagues

As mentioned above, before the dissolution of the WPFL, a new notable women's football league, the National Women's Football League (NWFL), had already been formed. Although the league did not have the ambition to be a fully professional women's league like the WPFL had attempted to do, it had considerable growth and lasted longer. The NWFL began with seven teams, and its first season was in 1974. Among the initial teams were the Toledo Troopers, who had previously played for the WPFL and dominated the NWFL for several years, and other teams like the Detroit Demons, the Dallas Bluebonnets, and the Columbus Pacesetters. Due to the high level of participation and enthusiasm, the league grew over time and extended to additional US cities.

Throughout its entire history, up until its last season in 1988, the NWFL provided a venue for women to play competitive American football. As we'll see later, it also helped sustain interest in women's football throughout the period between the WPFL's 1973 collapse and the professional women's football league's subsequent rebirth in the late 1990s and early 2000s. Because of the NWFL, which set the stage for the sport's growth and development in the decades that followed, women's football and its players demonstrated their resilience throughout this time.

The NWFL had a reorganization of clubs throughout the 1980s, with the Columbus Pacesetters serving as a symbol of the league's continuity from its creation until its dissolution in 1988. It was during this decade that the Toledo Furies came into being. This team is a monument to the tenacity of former Toledo Troopers players who wanted to foster a new generation of female football players. The accomplishments of the Furies, which culminated in the NWFL Championship in 1984, served as a ray of light for the sport of women's football. The move of clubs like the Furies into flag football by the year 1989, on the other hand, highlighted the fragile survival of women's professional football leagues in the face of financial restrictions and a diminishing fan base.

In this interim period, there were also other women's football leagues that contributed to keeping the interest in the female side of the sport alive, although they didn't have very large sizes. In parallel with the NWFL, it existed for a brief period in the Western States Women's Professional Football League from 1978 to 1980.

The Legacy of the 20th Century Leagues

Through the WPFL and the other leagues of the 20th century, the tale of women's football has been recounted. This narrative depicts the relentless struggle and ultimate resilience of female players in a sport that is dominated by male athletes. Despite the fact that the leagues faced tremendous financial and cultural obstacles, they represented an unrelenting effort to achieve gender equality in sports.

Looking at the financial difficulties that the women's leagues experienced, a more widespread problem in women's sports comes to light: the lack of investment and patience that their male counterparts enjoy. Despite the fact that the myth of sports teams as "cavernous money pits" applies without discrimination, rich supporters are often found in men's franchises who are ready to tolerate early losses in exchange for future returns. A systematic undervaluing of women's sports is shown by the discrepancy in financial support and cultural value that exists between the two parties.

Of course, one could answer that sponsors and investors act according to the public's preferences and the return their investments are expected to have. So, this is not to accuse anyone of their choices but to point out a basic problem women's sports often have to face. Ultimately, only society's interest and appreciation in women's sports can resolve this problem, and helping to raise interest is what this book is all about.

In spite of these obstacles, the women's leagues and their teams were able to demonstrate the various capabilities of female athletes, therefore challenging preconceptions and increasing the number of women who participate in sports. The presence of the leagues at a period of significant progress toward gender equality in the United

States acted as a direct challenge to the perception that women did not belong in football or that their involvement was purely a show.

The Role of the Media

It's difficult to overstate the importance of media coverage in creating public opinion and support for women's football, as well as how little coverage exists. The mainstream media's previous mistreatment of women's football, as well as their contempt for the sport, played a significant role in the sport's battle for survival and legitimacy. However, the advent of social media and heightened awareness of gender disparities in sports have begun to change the narrative. This has made it possible for female athletes to engage directly with fans and campaign for their sport.

Essentially, the progression of women's football from the leagues of previous decades to the leagues that exist now is a representation of a larger fight for equality, recognition, and respect in the sporting world. This highlights the need to maintain lobbying efforts, make investments, and bring about cultural reforms in order to guarantee that women's sports are viewed not as novelty sports but rather as essential components of the athletic landscape.

The Second Women's Professional Football League (1999-2007)

In 1999, a new ground-breaking program was launched that upended the established order and made it possible for female players to show off their skills on the gridiron: the Professional American Football League (WPFL). The founders were two businessmen, Carter Turner and Terry Sullivan. The new WPFL was not connected t older league with the same name we talked about above the vision of developing women's American football to level, breaking boundaries and prejudices and providing a new setting for female athletes.

The league began its adventure in American professional sports with just two teams: the Minnesota Vixens and the Lake Michigan Minx. The first game of the WPFL was played in the Hubert H. Humphrey Metrodome in Minneapolis, Minnesota. It had great success, which gave the new league an awesome starting point from which to grow. A straightforward demonstration match gave way to the "No Limits" Barnstorming Tour, a six-game tour featuring the nation's best female athletes that captivated crowds and raised awareness of women's football.

Those initial successes allowed the WPFL to expand right away and begin its first season in 2000, with 11 teams from around the United States. But the first season had its challenges. The league had financial and organizational instability, which caused chaos and resulted in a shorter regular season as well as claims of unpaid player pay.

The challenges did not stop the league from continuing its development. Although the two founders left the organization very early, the WPFL experienced a significant restructuring in 2001. With the founders of the league out, it was the franchise owners Melissa Korpacz, Dee Kennamer, Robin Howington, and Donna Roebuck who planned and implemented the needed changes as the league was growing and demonstrated it had potential. These modifications, which ushered in a new phase of expansion and prosperity, included shifting the season start from autumn to July and modifying player remuneration.

Over the course of its existence, the WPFL has attracted national attention by showcasing the extraordinary skill and commitment of female athletes via exciting championship contests. Every championship game, from Houston Energy's domination to the Dallas Diamonds' and SoCal Scorpions' victories, served as a monument to the talent, tenacity, and fervor of women in football.

The WPFL challenged prejudices and provided inspiration for future generations of female athletes as it grew in popularity and prominence, leaving an enduring legacy in the sport. Despite the league's 2007 closure, its legacy lives on as a source of opportunity and empowerment for female American football players.

In hindsight, the Women's Professional American Football League transformed the sport and showed that a person's gender need not be a barrier to success in the NFL. Let's remember the WPFL's groundbreaking work and pioneering attitude as we honor the accomplishments of women in sports. Their influence may still be felt in the football community and beyond.

CHAPTER 4:

Current Landscape of Women in American Football

—◆—

The Women's Football Alliance and Other Current Leagues

The dissolution of the second attempt for a fully professional women's American football league did not leave American sports lacking women's football. The 21st century has been, since the beginning, more favorable toward women's sports than the previous one, and more women's football leagues followed. First, in parallel with the WPFL, the Independent Women's Football League (IWFL) was founded in 2000 and was functional until 2018. Second, other semi-professional leagues formed in the following years.

The IWFL was founded by female players with the intention of establishing a platform that would be solely devoted to female athletes competing in the sport. The league functioned in parallel with the WPFL until 2007, and then it kept the interest in women's football alive as the older existing league had done until the year 2018 when it dissolved. Initially, the IWFL was established by members of the Austin Outlaws franchise, Sandra Plato, Laurie Frederick, and Jaime

Bailey. One of the characteristics that exemplify the spirit of commitment and enthusiasm for the game that existed in this league, which was comprised of amateur and semi-professional players, is the fact that participants often bore a portion of their expenditures.

Three other notable women's leagues of American football were founded in recent years. These are the Women's Football Alliance (WFA), which was founded in 2009 and is currently the biggest one; the Women's National Football Conference (WNFC), founded in 2019; and the United States Women's Football League (USWFL), founded in 2009 which was initially an exhibition and spring league.

As mentioned above, the WFA is the biggest active women's American football league, so its importance and impact on the female side of the game are undoubtedly essential. The WFA has promoted inclusion and persistence in addition to offering a stage for athletic achievement. The league is owned and run by Jeff King and Lisa Gibbons King, and its base is in Exeter, California. Their goal is to highlight the commitment and fervor that define women's football. The WFA has been committed to removing obstacles within the sport of football and increasing the number of women who participate in the sport since it was founded.

The three competitive divisions in the WFA—Pro, Division 2, and Division 3—showcase the league's dedication to providing opportunities to players of all ability levels. This approach creates a supportive atmosphere for the development of skill and sportsmanship by guaranteeing that each player has the opportunity to compete at a level appropriate to her abilities and try to grow as much as possible. In addition, the WFA International program has allowed the league to reach a wider audience outside of the US with women's American football.

With 36 teams at launch, the WFA combined new teams with well-established clubs from previous leagues to demonstrate the ambition and cohesion of women's football. Remarkable occasions, like the league's first championship game in New Orleans and the championship games held at recognizable NFL stadiums, draw attention to the league's accomplishments and its stature in the eyes of the wider sports world.

Momentous anniversaries such as Whitney Zelee reaching 2,000 yards of running in a season and Allison Cahill reaching 100 quarterback touchdowns highlight the exceptional quality in the league. These successes encourage future generations of female athletes in addition to honoring individual greatness.

Notable events in the history of the league include the introduction of the W Bowl as the WFA National Championship game, the expansion of the league to include 65 teams in 2017 and collaborations with television networks that have increased the profile of women's football. An age of acknowledgment and gratitude for the contributions made by women to American football has begun, as shown by broadcast agreements and the backing of prominent sponsors, which highlight the sport's increasing interest and investment.

Beyond the pitch, the WFA has an effect on how society views women in sports and their advocacy for gender equality. The WFA continues to empower women, dispel preconceptions, and open doors for the next generation of female football players through tenacity, devotion, and community support.

The WFA is steadfast in its dedication to developing talent, creating opportunities, and elevating women's football to a significant position in the sports world. Women's American football's persistent energy and promise are shown by the league's continued success stories, both on and off the field. In the future, the WFA aims to continue to be dedicated to growing the sport of women's football and offering chances for players to further their careers. It continues to motivate women of all ages to follow their love for football and to redefine what is possible in the world of sports.

The WNFC is another essential factor in the development of women's football. The league consists of several teams in many locations in the United States, such as the Chicago Blitz, the Atlanta Phoenix, the Denver Bandits, and more. On the other hand, the United States Women's Football League (USWFL) is composed of two divisions, namely the North Division and the South Division. Additionally, the USWFL features a number of teams located in different locations, like the Michigan Queens, the Detroit Prowl, and the South Carolina Scorpions, amongst others. There is a significant number of women who enjoy competing at an organized level, and the female version of football continues its path of development and aims to achieve greater recognition and respect in the world of sports. Despite the fact that a major professional women's football league has not been able to consolidate in the American sports industry, the constant presence and continuous appearance of new leagues demonstrate that there is a significant number of women who enjoy competing at an organized level.

A Provocative Idea: The Lingerie Football League

Among the various professional and semi-professional women's football leagues that exist, there is one indoor women's league with notable commercial success and a provocative setting. This league poses a series of interesting and thought-provoking questions and can spark debates: the Extreme Football League or simply X League.

The X League was founded in 2009 as the Lingerie Football League. In 2013, its name changed to the Legends Football League, and since 2019, it has operated under the name X League. The provocative innovation of the X League is evident in its initial name, the Lingerie Football League. In this league, women play dressed in sexy outfits and with hot makeup, as the league's idea is to emphasize not only the game of football but also the feminine side of the players.

Many men like to watch the X League's games for obvious reasons, but one can easily note that there are also many women in the stands who enjoy the spectacle and the different and humorous vibe of the league. We must add that as fun as it sounds, the women who play in the X League are real football players, and their games are perfectly competitive and tough full-contact football games, not a show but a real sport.

The X League is also very interesting in the context of this book, as it reveals theoretical problems and different perspectives on superficially common grounds: is the X League setting a promotion of women's sports, or does it objectify women and portray them in a sexualized manner that has nothing to do with sports and gender equality and instead conserves a certain image of femininity? On the other hand, why would displaying and celebrating the female body in the context of football be diminishing for women? Should women who play football look like men to be accepted as real athletes?

Advocating political, social, and economic freedom, we should defend any initiative that promotes sports and women's sports, as far as the players freely choose to participate and the safety standards are met.

An Idea for the Future

Returning to traditional full-contact football, the two most important women's American football leagues in the 2020s, the WFA and the WNFC, although less commercial than the X League, have also grown in popularity and media coverage, reaching a level that the women's football leagues had never enjoyed in the past. Although they remain semi-professional and not fully professional, the growth in popularity and media coverage also brings more commercial sponsors, as well as the interest and endorsements of famous athletes and stars.

Yet, if women's football is going to attain its full potential, it could be necessary to have a unified league format that is comparable to the merger between the AFL and the NFL or the structure of the WNBA. There is the potential for such consolidation to promote sustainability, make it possible to compensate players fairly, and increase fan involvement. Despite the progress that has been accomplished, women's football continues to find itself confronted with challenges. One of these challenges is the absence of institutional support at the educational level. This highlights the need for ongoing lobbying and structural adjustments in order to guarantee the development and recognition of the sport.

The players, teams, and leagues that are developing women's football are not only paving the way for the growth of the sport, but they are also questioning and rewriting the narrative that surrounds women in sports. This is happening as women's football moves forward into the future.

Jennifer Welter: An Authentic Pioneer for Women in American Football

As far as American football is concerned, Jennifer Welter is a name that is associated with shattering boundaries. She was born on October 27, 1977, and she has had an indelible effect on the sport. She has broken past limits and redefined what it means to be a coach and player in a field that has historically been controlled by males. She has opened the way for many women to follow in her footsteps.

Welter played for 13 years in women's football teams with great success and was also a member of the USA national team that won the World Championships in 2010 and 2013. Nevertheless, she became known nationwide mostly when the Texas Revolution team of the Champions Indoor Football League signed her as a running back in 2014. That was a big deal, as until then, women had only played the positions of placekicker or kicker in men's professional football teams. Welter was acknowledged as a pioneer in the sport for her perseverance and talent on the field.

After a year, she made history again by becoming the first female NFL coaching intern when she joined the Arizona Cardinals, marking the start of her career as a professional football coach. Her revolutionary moment on the sidelines during the team's training camp and preseason had a lasting influence on the American football community, upending long-held beliefs and motivating a great number of people.

Beyond her role as a player and coach in the NFL, Welter has many other accomplishments. She has, of course, played in several women's football teams, such as the Dallas Dragons and the Dallas Diamonds, where she distinguished herself as a player so talented and capable as to be considered and then included in men's football. Welter demonstrated her abilities on the world stage as well, which helped her establish herself as one of the sport's elite competitors over time. In fact, as noted above, she competed for the United States and won gold in the 2010 and 2013 Women's Football World Championships run by the International Federation of American Football.

Moreover, Welter's impact transcends the boundaries of the football field since she is not only a great sportswoman but also a notable scholar at the academic level and very active as an entrepreneur. In addition to her accomplishments as a football player and coach, she holds a Ph.D. in psychology from Capella University and a further specialization in sports psychology, as she holds a master's degree in that field; she also received the Women's Entrepreneurship Day Pioneer Award for her substantial contribution and trailblazing efforts in the sports industry. Her participation in Mogul's Women's History Month #IAmAMogul campaign highlighted her position as a change agent and encouraged people to defy expectations and follow their interests with courage.

In that respect, Jennifer Welter's legacy is a source of inspiration and hope as it shows how someone with competence, endurance, and dedication can make their way in an area that was previously off-limits to women. Objectively, she opened a totally new avenue to female athletes and coaches, with two breakthroughs on the gridiron as a player and on the sidelines as a coach. But even before that, her career and accomplishments as a player in women's American football secured her place as a legendary figure of the female side of the sport.

Touchdowns and Triumphs: Sam Gordon's Game-Changing Impact on Women's Football

In the year 2012, a little girl by the name of Sam Gordon broke preconceptions and captivated the attention of the whole country with her remarkable performance in the Utah PeeWee Football League.

Gordon demonstrated her skill on the football field by not just participating but also succeeding. She scored 25 touchdowns and made 65 tackles, demonstrating her capabilities. It was not a brief flash of popularity that she achieved but rather a trigger for a profound transformation in the landscape of women's football. Her success went viral. In addition to being a tale about Sam's personal accomplishments, it is also a story about transformation, persistence, and the shattering of boundaries that have been in place for a very long time.

As Sam has progressed from being a viral phenomenon to becoming a famous person in women's sports, she has maintained an unflinching devotion to the sport that she really enjoys playing. Gordon has exploited her position to push for more inclusion in football, and she has done so by speaking with legends like Gloria Steinem and earning the first NFL Honors Game Changer Award in 2018. Her point is very obvious and powerful: Young women like football and should be given every chance to participate in the sport.

Gordon, upon becoming aware of the lack of chances available to young girls in the sport of football, decided to take things into her own hands. She was the pioneer in the United States of America, establishing the Utah Girls Tackling Football League, which was the first all-girls tackling league. This demonstrates the demand for the activity among young girls as well as their excitement for it. The league began with just fifty players and has now expanded to include over six hundred participants. This program, in conjunction with the backing of Under Armour, highlights a major change toward recognizing and promoting female players in the sport of football.

A watershed event in the history of women's sports has been marked by the support of Under Armour, which includes the introduction of women's football cleats and the sponsorship of the Utah Girls Tackle

Football League. It is a demonstration of how attitudes are shifting toward women in football and becoming more accepting. The efforts of Gordon have not only made it possible for young girls to participate in the sport, but they have also dispelled some of the most common prejudices that exist around women in the sport.

The transition from improvised equipment to cleats specifically built for women's football is illustrative of the development that has been accomplished over the course of time. To give young women a taste of the fantasy that has traditionally been reserved for their male counterparts, Gordon's league provides them with the opportunity to play under the lights at Rice-Eccles Stadium, which is located on the campus of the University of Utah. An important step toward achieving equality in sports, this highlights the fact that the excitement of the game is not dependent on a person's gender.

Nevertheless, despite these developments, difficulties continue to exist. One of the most widespread problems of gender inequality in sports is brought to light by the absence of a defined route for female football players. As a result of the fact that women do not have access to comparable high school and college football programs fifty years after Title IX was passed, it is clear that there are structural hurdles that continue to restrict chances for female athletes. A deeper understanding of the challenges involved in establishing actual equality in sports is shown by Gordon's criticism of the execution of Title IX.

Prominent Female Football Players

Besides Jennifer Welter and Sam Gordon, there are several other influential women in the world of American football. For example, Patricia Palinkas became the first woman to play in the Atlantic Coast

Football League in 1970 as the holder for the Orlando Panthers. Katie Hnida, another groundbreaking player, became the kicker for the Fort Wayne FireHawks in the Continental Indoor Football League in 2010. Their contributions have paved the way for women in football, demonstrating that the sport is not just limited to men.

Additionally, the recent achievements and roles of women in various aspects of American football highlight the ongoing progress toward gender equality in the sport. For instance, Toni Harris stands out for being the first woman to receive a college football scholarship at a position other than kicker, playing as a safety for East Los Angeles College before signing with Central Methodist University. Her pursuit of a master's degree in criminal justice, along with coaching youth football clinics, showcases her multifaceted involvement in the sport and beyond.

Exploring the history of women's football, it's clear that the sport is full of influential players who have significantly shaped its landscape. Brittany Bushman, for instance, has been an impactful player, demonstrating her skill and resilience through a remarkable career. After becoming the 2012 WFA MVP and playing for Team USA in the 2013 World Championships, Bushman faced a setback due to an injury but made a triumphant return to the field in 2018 with the Texas Elite Spartans, eventually playing for the 2022 WNFC Championship.

Another notable figure is Cynthia "Red" Bryant, a veteran player from the Minnesota Vixen, who has been involved in women's football for over two decades. As one of the original players from the 1999 season that restarted organized women's tackle football in the U.S. after the NWFL folded in the late '80s, Bryant's story is one of dedication and passion for the sport. Despite facing challenges, she has continued to play and inspire, highlighting her commitment to football.

These players, among many others, demonstrate the depth of talent and resilience in women's football. Their contributions not only highlight the physical capabilities and achievements of women in the sport but also reflect the broader cultural shift toward gender equality in athletics. Their stories of overcoming barriers, combined with their exceptional talent, have paved the way for future generations of female football players, underscoring the importance of visibility and support for women in sports.

Is Feminism Incompatible With Football?

Arab-American activist Lina AbiRafeh examines the intricate link between a sport that is entrenched in hyper-masculinity, such as American football, and the continuous search for gender equality in a thought-provoking investigation of the interactions that exist between feminism and football. Her experience at a football game, in which she was met with sexist insults and was surrounded by a largely male crowd, serves as a discouraging background for her inquiry: Is it possible for feminism to find a home in the world of football, which has historically been associated with men?

AbiRafeh makes the observation that football is not only a game but also a cultural phenomenon that encompasses and maintains gender norms. The normal football-watching experience, in which males are in the spotlight and women are relegated to the sidelines, would be a reflection of larger cultural standards that feminists have been working to undermine for a long time. According to AbiRafeh's somewhat extreme view, there is a widespread misogyny that taints the football sport, which is shown by the nasty remarks that are made about cheerleaders during games as well as the objectification of cheerleaders.

AbiRafeh recognizes the existence of outliers and the unquestionable potential of female players who strive to enter this male-dominated arena despite the fact that it depicts football culture in a negative light. The establishment of women's football leagues, such as the Women's Football Alliance, represents a huge step toward inclusion despite the fact that it is still in its infancy. AbiRafeh talks about what she considers huge salary differences and financial constraints that are imposed on female players, which, on the other hand, underline the persistent difficulties that must be overcome in order to successfully achieve real equality within the sport.

Her mention of the former "Lingerie Football League," now called X League, brings to light not the excessive objectification and commercialization of women's bodies under the cover of sport, as she thinks, but rather that she doesn't really grasp how the economy and sports industry works and the simple fact that one should sell something that others want to buy, in order to make money. She struggles to reconcile the fact that the X League encourages and promotes women's sports while at the same time benefiting from the "sexualization" of female athletes. One could say the same exact thing for male boxers and MMA fighters, who fight practically semi-nude and obviously often could look sexy to heterosexual women or homosexual men. Finding a way to make a version of women's football more appealing is something a league should get credit for, not be criticized for.

There has been some progress made in the promotion of gender equality in football, with programs targeted at boosting the number of women who are employed in administrative, scouting, and coaching positions. As AbiRafeh points out, however, the entrenched culture of male dominance that exists throughout football organizations presents substantial hurdles to these initiatives. The topic of whether or not women are secure in such settings continues to be a significant worry, which highlights the need for a culture transformation that tackles issues of sexism, harassment, and violence.

It is further complicated by the fact that football intersects with social concerns such as domestic violence, and the link between feminism and the sport is more complicated. At the same time as AbiRafeh draws attention to the worrying link between football games and the rise in domestic violence episodes, she raises significant concerns about the accountability of sports leagues and the culture that they propagate.

There are glimmerings of optimism for a future in football that is more inclusive and equal despite the hurdles that have been presented. The recent accomplishments in women's soccer serve as a model for what is feasible in football and other sports today. The route toward reconciling feminism with football, however, is plagued with challenges and calls for a deliberate effort to demolish the established gender standards that now characterize the sport. This is the conclusion that AbiRafeh draws.

In conclusion, AbiRafeh's musings on the compatibility or incompatibility of feminism with football spark an important discussion on the need to institute structural reform inside the sport. As the sport of football continues to develop, the goal of gender equality continues to be a major problem that requires attention, action, and, eventually, a reinvention of what the sport may and should represent.

CHAPTER 5:

Breaking Barriers: Women in Coaching

—◆—

The fact that female coaches have worked full-time for NFL teams in recent years, something that had never happened before 2016, is an evident sign of a change in the great American football league's dynamics. That did not happen by chance, but it's a product of the developments we talked about in the previous chapters, which saw women enter and be accepted into the world of football with more consistency and determination. The NFL took note of those developments and opened itself up to women and the notions of diversity and inclusivity. The new conditions give hope that after other sectors and sports, American football will also be a sport where women's presence and activity will look and be totally normal.

The year 2016 was a significant turning point in the NFL's march toward becoming more open to women. It was the year when the Buffalo Bills made an unprecedented choice, that is, hiring a woman as a full-time coach, Kathryn Smith. She would work for the team as a special quality control coach. The breakthrough accomplishment of Kathryn Smith established the groundwork for later milestones we'll talk about in the following paragraphs and pages, as this shift was the beginning of more opportunities for women to work in coaching jobs for NFL teams.

Another significant year for women's participation in the NFL was 2021, when 12 women were regularly employed as coaches by NFL clubs starting that season and continuing until the spring of 2024. This is an incredible accomplishment for both the NFL and football-loving women, demonstrating that a competent candidate's gender is no longer a barrier to joining the coaching staff of the league.

The 12 female coaches of the NFL as of April 2024 are:

- Angela Baker, New York Giants Offensive Assistant Coach.
- Callie Brownson, Cleveland Browns Assistant Wide Recei.
- Kaelyn Buskey, Baltimore Ravens Assistant Strength and Conditioning.
- Jill Costanza, Detroit Lions Director of Sports Science.
- Isabel Diaz, Indianapolis Colts Special Teams Coaching Fellow.
- Maral Javadifar, Tampa Bay Buccaneers Director of Rehabilitation/

Performance Coach.

- Jennifer King, Chicago Bears Assistant Running Backs Coach.
- Autumn Lockwood, Philadelphia Eagles Associate Performance Coach.
- Lori Locust, Tennessee Titans Defensive Quality Control Coach.
- Haley Roberts, Tennessee Titans Assistant Sports Performance Coach.
- Megan Rosburg, Baltimore Ravens Assistant to the Head Coach.
- Marianna Salas, Baltimore Ravens Coaching Research Fellow.
- Moderated by MJ Acosta-Ruiz, NFL Network Talent.

In the following sections of this chapter, we will discuss a few of these trailblazing women coaches in more detail and point out some essential milestones in the unfolding of this process.

Lori Locust and Maral Javadifar: First Women to Win the Super Bowl

Lori Locust's Atypical and Extraordinary Path to Greatness

In an environment so dominated by rough athleticism as professional American football, Lori Locust has been a quiet force, managing to mark the sport's history and especially coaching history. Locust's journey from her childhood in Philadelphia, Pennsylvania, where she was born in 1964, to her position as a successful coach of the NFL is a demonstration of tenacity, perseverance, and one of the best examples of breaking down boundaries from the many of them we present in this book.

Lori Locust's initial experience with football came about as a result of the thriving sports culture that existed in her hometown of Harrisburg, Pennsylvania. She attended Temple University for a short period of time after graduating from Susquehanna Township High School in 1982. However, she was forced to quit her studies in order to take care of her sick father. So, she did not begin her journey into the world of football until the year 2004, when she was forty years old. That makes her story even more impactful, as she had to overcome additional family problems, and she had the determination to go after her goal to enter the sports world at an older age than usual. We may say that her whole career on the football field has been marked by talent and persistence.

At first, Locust played defensive lineman for the Central Pennsylvania Vipers, a semi-professional women's football club. She progressed through the ranks of the Vipers, winning the team captaincy and MVP award in her fourth season. She regrettably had a knee injury later on, which finally prompted her to decide to give up playing. But while one narrative ended, a new one that would be much more significant for both her and American athletics started to emerge.

Locust took her expertise and passion for the football field to the sidelines, making the transition from player to coach as smooth as possible. She set out on a journey of coaching, and her career is nothing short of amazing so far, beginning with her post-retirement coaching of her Vipers team and continuing with stops at Susquehanna Township High School and then men's amateur teams, such as the Central Penn Piranha and the Baltimore Ravens.

Locust's name was written into the books of American football's history already in March 2019, when she became just the first woman to be hired as a position coach and only the third to be hired as a full-time assistant coach by an NFL team. But the event that will make her remembered for generations to come happened almost two years later, on February 7, 2021. Working as a defensive line coach for the Tampa Bay Buccaneers under head coach Bruce Arians, Locust became the first woman to ever win the Super Bowl and become NFL champion, along with her colleague Maral Javadifar, whom we will meet in the next section.

Fast forward two more years, and on February 5, 2023, the Tennessee Titans hired Locust as a defensive assistant coach, confirming her successful career and her efficiency as an NFL coach during the previous seasons.

Not only does Lori Locust's story inspire women hoping to pursue a career in football, but it can also act as a beacon of hope for anybody facing obstacles and misfortune while pursuing their career or personal objectives. Her legacy will endure as a tribute to her strength, ability, and tenacity as she continues to make her imprint on the football world. Not to be overlooked is the fact that her achievement was made possible not only by her pioneering role in a field that had previously been unwelcoming to women but also by the unique start to her football career and the challenges she overcame personally. It is evident that Locust's journey was not without difficulties and disappointments, but her unyielding tenacity and fortitude enabled her to overcome them and fulfill her ultimate ambition: becoming an NFL coach.

Using her own story of beginning in a semi-professional women's football league in Harrisburg, Pennsylvania, Locust emphasizes how important it is to identify and nurture talent at the local level.

As Lori Locust married Andrew Locust, a former Temple football player, she also succeeded in balancing her family life with her thriving coaching profession. Together, they have two children.

Maral Javadifar's Journey to Glory

Maral Javadifar was born on March 17, 1990, to Iranian immigrants and, initially, it seemed that her sport would be basketball. Thanks to her height and ability, she played for the Pace University women's basketball team from 2008 to 2012, and she was also the team captain. The team was successful, making it to the NCAA tournament three consecutive times and reaching the Sweet 16 phase in 2011. Yet, for all her successful college basketball career, Javadifar was meant to make history in American football.

At Pace University, Maral Javadifar got a bachelor's degree in molecular biology, and then she continued her studies at New York Medical College, obtaining a Ph.D. in Physical Therapy in 2015. She worked as a physical therapist and a performance trainer and completed her Sports Physical Therapy Residency at Virginia Commonwealth University in 2018. Her work extends beyond the clinic and the field, contributing as a guest lecturer at George Mason University.

Thanks to her excellent academic and working bases, she was hired in March 2019 by the Tampa Bay Buccaneers to be their assistant strength and conditioning coach. That made her one of the first female full-time coaches in NFL history. At the same time, the Tampa Bay Buccaneers became the first team with two female coaches since they already had hired Lori Locust, as we saw in the previous subchapter.

The female duo of the Buccaneers would complete this tale of inclusivity and overcoming old barriers and prejudices in the most fabulous way, as they were both parts of the team that won the Super Bowl on February 7, 2021. This milestone is not just a personal achievement for Javadifar and Locust but one of the beacons of the progress made over the last decades and years; it will always symbolize a future where gender is no longer a barrier to entry and the possibility of earning success, even in a sport that used to be almost unbearable for women.

It is worth mentioning that the first two women who won the Super Bowl both had additional disadvantages and barriers that needed to be overcome in order to reach professional success and enter the path that eventually brought them together to that historic accomplishment. We saw that Locust had early family problems that made her stop her college studies, and she started playing football as an amateur after she was 40 years old. In Javadifar's case, we should not forget to mention her Iranian heritage and the struggles her family faced migrating to the United States or the limits and prohibitions her mother had previously experienced living under the theocratic Iranian regime. Maral Javadifar made those obstacles and experiences into a source of inspiration and determination to seize every opportunity and even challenge societal norms.

Her impact goes beyond her job in taking care of the players' physical condition and contributing to their tactical preparation; she represents the evolving landscape of American football, where diversity, equality, and excellence are not mutually exclusive but interwoven. As the NFL and other sports organizations continue to embrace change, Javadifar's journey to glory will undoubtedly inspire future generations of women in sports.

Callie Brownson: Excellency Inside and on the Side of the Gridiron

Callie Brownson was born in Mount Vernon, Virginia, on October 15, 1989. Her father, Bruce B. Brownson, was the person who raised her, and obviously, he introduced her to the magic and excitement of sports and American football. She was passionate about sports, and she used to play softball at Mount Vernon High School, not football, because there was no girls' football at her high school, and the boy's team didn't let girls join. Nevertheless, Callie Brownson was not demoralized; instead, she quickly followed her talent and passion for football right after graduation.

At 19, while she had begun studying at George Mason University, she successfully joined the D.C. Divas of the Women's Football Alliance, making her dream of becoming a football player come true. Not only did she play with the Divas for eight seasons, but she also had great success, being one of the best female players on the gridiron. She was named All-American four times and was the team captain in five seasons. Most importantly, Brownson was selected to enter the United States national team. They won two gold medals at the Women's World

Championships organized by the International Federation of American Football in 2013 and 2017.

Brownson's coaching career would be equally remarkable, and it started very early, during her active years as a player. Already at age 21, in parallel with her playing career at the Women's Football Alliance league and the international stage as a national team member, she started working as an assistant coach for the football team of her high school, Mount Vernon High School. She worked there for three seasons. In 2017, with her playing career, having reached the women's American football summit and already having coaching experience, she was hired by the New York Jets as a scouting intern, entering the NFL.

But her next professional step in the gridiron football world would be even more important. In September 2018, after a short period as an intern, she became the first woman to be hired as a full-time NCAA Division I coach at Dartmouth College.

In 2019, Brownson returned to the NFL after the Buffalo Bills hired her as a coaching intern. Finally, on November 29, 2020, she became the first woman to coach a position group in the NFL regular season, filling in for tight ends coach Drew Petzing of the Cleveland Browns in the week 12 game against the Jacksonville Jaguars. Then, during the week 17 game against the Pittsburgh Steelers, she filled in for passing game coordinator and wide receivers coach Chad O'Shea. During Cleveland's first game in the 2020-21 playoffs, she filled in again for coach Drew Petzing.

In May 2021, Brownson was arrested for driving with her blood alcohol content significantly over the limit. The Browns suspended her from team activities, requiring her to face discipline. Nevertheless, Brownson was soon back at her job and remains a valuable member of the Cleveland Browns.

On February 27, 2024, Brownson was one of the 12 women who participated in the opening panel of the NFL Women's Forum at the 2024 NFL Combine. They are the 12 women who work as coaches for NFL teams, which is even more remarkable if we consider that, as Samantha Rapoport, NFL Senior Director of Diversity and Inclusion, said when the program started eight years ago, zero women were working in full-time coaching jobs. The progress made during these years is impressive, and Callie Brownson is one of the central figures in this development.

Jennifer King: First Black Female NFL Coach

Jennifer King is another remarkable pioneer in the field of professional American football, as she became the first black female full-time assistant coach in the NFL's history. Her promotion to the position of assistant running back coach for the Washington Commanders in 2021 marked a significant moment in women's sports history, especially important for black women.

Born on August 6, 1984, in Eden, North Carolina, King played basketball and softball during her college years at Guilford College, where she got her degree in sports management. After graduating from college in 2006, King joined the Carolina Phoenix team of the Women's Football Alliance and played as a quarterback and wide receiver for 11 consecutive years until 2017. Then, she played in the 2018 season for the New York Sharks, where she won the WFA Division II championship. Finally, she played for the D.C. Divas in the 2019 season.

In parallel with her career as a football player, King continued her studies and also earned a Master of Science degree in sports management. Interestingly, from 2006 to 2016, she also worked as an assistant coach for the basketball team of Greensboro College. The results were notably successful, as the team made the NCAA tournament four times, won five regular season titles and two conference titles, and had an overall record of 182 wins and 63 wins during her years as an assistant coach. Her participation in a successful project gave her the opportunity to become the head coach of the Johnson & Wales University women's basketball team. She worked there for two seasons, and her success was even more impressive, as the team won the USCAA Division II National Championship.

It's evident that King has a great love for athletics in general, having played and worked on different sports and studied sports management. Her contemporaneous success in basketball as a coach, in football as a player, and in education as an academic student is extraordinary, and it was already enough for her to be seen as an inspiring example for many people inside and outside football and sports. However, King's most groundbreaking accomplishment was yet to come. In 2018, she was hired by the Carolina Panthers of the NFL as an intern coach and then as a full-time assistant coach of the wide receivers by the Arizona Hotshots team of the Alliance of American Football league. In 2019, she returned to the NFL and the Panthers as an intern running backs coach and also an offensive assistant at Dartmouth College. Having established herself in the field of men's football, King was hired in 2020 as an intern by the Washington Football Team, and finally, coach Ron Rivera promoted her to full-time assistant running backs coach in 2021, marking, as already said, the first time a black woman became a full-time coach in the NFL. In 2024 King is still an NFL coach, working as an offensive assistant for the Chicago Bears.

Kathryn Smith's Journey to Becoming the NFL's First Full-Time Female Coach

Kathryn Smith was born in the mid-1980s in DeWitt, a suburb of Syracuse, New York. She would go on to become the first full-time female coach in the history of the NFL, almost a century after the foundation of the league.

Smith began her journey into the heart of American football in her birth town DeWitt, where she attended Christian Brothers Academy and graduated in 2003. Then, she attended St. John's University in New York City, where she majored in sports management because, since her childhood, she was passionate about sports and was certain that she wanted to follow a career in the sports industry as a manager of teams and sports organizations. During her studies, she engaged herself deeper in sports, becoming a student manager for the institution's men's basketball team.

In parallel, she had already begun working in the NFL since 2003 through internships, which laid the groundwork for her unprecedented ascension to coaching. Her first job was for the New York Jets as an intern for game-day and special events. This position gave her the opportunity to gain first-hand experience with the activities of the NFL. By 2005, she had completed her internship with the Jets as a college scouting intern, which allowed her to further deepen her knowledge of the game and the players.

In 2007, Smith was promoted to the role of player personnel assistant, a post she held until 2013. This promotion was a result of her devotion and hard work, which paid off. Smith was able to acquire a great amount of information and experience throughout her time with the

Jets, which she brought with her when she made the transition to her current position as an administrative assistant.

The year 2015 was a key turning point in Smith's professional life when she accepted a position as an administrative assistant with the Buffalo Bills team, but what followed was a turning point not only for her personally but for the entire American football and sports world. On January 20, 2016, the Bills organization gave her the job of special quality control coach of the team, making her the first woman to ever be in a full-time coaching position in the NFL.

Working under the guidance of head coach Rex Ryan, Smith was responsible for doing a thorough analysis of the performance of the Bills' special teams, developing strategies for making improvements and providing assistance with game planning. This is an essential part of football that is frequently overlooked by casual observers.

The departure of Rex Ryan from the Bills resulted in Smith not being retained by the new coach, Sean McDermott, prior to the start of the 2017 season. However, Kathryn Smith's influence on the NFL and on female coaches cannot be overstated, despite the fact that her tenure as a full-time NFL coach was relatively brief, only for one season. Other women in the league were able to follow in Smith's footsteps thanks to her pioneering work that opened possibilities that previously had never existed for women on the biggest stage of American football. Right away, in the 2017 season, another woman was hired as a full-time coach in the NFL by the San Francisco 49ers. She was Katie Sowers, who we are going to meet in the following section.

A new generation of women are inspired and determined to pursue their aspirations in professional football following the road that Kathryn Smith first managed to take, creating a beacon of progress as the NFL continues to undergo its ongoing evolution. It is a reminder of the transformational power of determination, hard effort, and the willingness to challenge the status quo. The fact that Smith was able to break through the glass ceiling in one of the most male-dominated industries in sports during the course of his career is a credit to her dogged determination.

Katie Sowers: the First Woman to Reach the Super Bowl

Katie Sowers was born in Hesston, Kansas, on August 7, 1986, and was raised in a neighborhood with strong Mennonite beliefs. She got involved with football early on, demonstrating from the youngest age one could think of a strong love for the sport. Sowers's early years in Hesston prepared her for her career aspirations. She began playing American football at the youthful age of eight, already displaying her talent and tenacity.

She attended Heston College and Goshen College, and in 2012, she got her master's degree in kinesiology at the University of Central Missouri in 2012. Thus, as in other cases we've seen and will see later, too, Sowers had a strong educational background in sports science, which is important to point out. It shows that successful sportswomen and sportsmen are not driven only by an entertainment-oriented approach to sports but by a passion for studies and knowledge of sports at a scientific level.

After she completed her academic studies, Sowers joined the Kansas City Titans of the Women's Football Alliance, becoming a football player at the most important current women's league. Later, she played for West Michigan Mayhem. Her on-field skill was unequivocal, and it culminated with her helping the US women's national football team win the 2013 IFAF Women's World Championship as a teammate of Jennifer Welter and other women footballers we've mentioned or will talk about later in the book.

Having earned her post among the best women players, Sowers got unlucky, as she had a hip injury that ended her playing career in 2016. She immediately took action, and during the same year, she interned as a wide receivers coach with the Atlanta Falcons, where she started her NFL coaching career. The next step was the most important, as she was hired by the San Francisco 49ers in 2017 in the position of full-time offensive assistant coach. There, she was about to make history when, in the 2019 season, the team reached the Super Bowl LIV, and Sowers became the first woman to ever reach the NFL's title game as a coaching staff member.

In the 2021 season, Sowers joined the Kansas City Chiefs, and after that, she became Ottawa University's director of athletic strategic initiatives and head coach of the university's women's flag football team.

Finally, another point that should be mentioned about Katie Sowers is that she made the choice to come out as openly lesbian, which apart from the rest, made her also the first LGBT coach in the NFL. So, in her case, overcoming old boundaries and opening football and sports to social groups that once would be seen as aliens in the football world also has a second meaning. Her example promotes representation and equality in football, encouraging numerous people to follow their aspirations regardless of their gender or sexual orientation.

College Coaching: Mini Bolden-Morris

Mini Bolden-Morris is the first woman to become a graduate assistant coach in college football in a top conference institution since Carol White worked with Georgia Tech kickers in the late 1980s. As the first woman in such a coaching job position in decades, Mimi Bolden-Morris stands out as a pioneer in the world of college football and, generally, American football. Not only has her incredible transition from the basketball floor to the gridiron garnered a lot of attention, but it has also served as a source of motivation for a great number of people all around the country. The essential role that Bolden-Morris played brings to light the progress that is being made in the direction of encouraging more gender diversity and inclusiveness in the sport.

From an early age, Bolden-Morris was involved in the sport of football since she was raised in Belle Glade, Florida, a community that is well-known for its extensive football legacy. She spent her childhood standing on the sidelines with her father and throwing footballs about. After managing a young flag football team during her last year at Georgetown University, she decided that teaching football was her ultimate ambition. Although she excelled in basketball and received awards at both Boston College and Georgetown University, she eventually decided that coaching football was her ultimate aim.

Bolden-Morris made history by becoming a member of the coaching staff of the Michigan Wolverines, which is now being coached by Jim Harbaugh, the national head coach. This extraordinary appointment was a milestone for Bolden-Morris professionally, but also a significant moment for all women in the football sector, players and coaches, like the other moments presented in this chapter. Her mother's effort, which consisted of reaching out to Coach Harbaugh on her behalf, was a significant factor in gaining the chance. This exemplifies the significance of advocating for oneself in order to achieve one's goals and objectives.

Bolden-Morris provides assistance to the offensive staff in the form of scouting reports, analyzes the techniques used by opponents, and provides support to the tight ends coach during games, therefore blending in smoothly with the coaching staff.

But her influence goes well beyond her function as a supportive coach. She has opened the road for future generations of women to follow in her footsteps by breaking prejudices and doggedly following their passion and contributed to the opening of new opportunities for women in sports.

The NFL's Commitment to Diversity

An indication of the NFL's dedication to diversity and inclusiveness is the growing number of female coaches. Dreaming big is not useless or counterproductive when one is determined to work really hard and study their favorite sport seriously. These accomplished women broke through barriers and became an inspiration to female athletes and coaches because of their unwavering commitment to excellence and, most importantly, their love for the game. All that became possible also because there has been a strong push to establish a more accessible route for women to pursue coaching positions in the NFL during the most recent times. By harnessing the expertise and skills of female coaches working in high school and youth programs, a remarkable chance emerges to foster a more inclusive pathway for coaching positions in the NFL.

A further increase in the number of women working in coaching roles in the NFL seems a reasonable expectation and perspective right now. Nevertheless, it is still hard to imagine a woman in a leadership role, such as a head coach instead of an assistant. On the other hand, that would be the wrong way to think about the issue. The point is for women to have equal opportunities and not be excluded or underestimated because of their gender. If women are to become head coaches in the NFL or other major professional sports, though, there should be first women capable of taking on such responsibility and, above all, reaching the highest level of knowing and understanding the game. The point is that giving women the opportunity to grow as players and coaches, as well as mentorship and support from fellow female coaches, can be critical. By sharing their experiences and knowledge, they empower each other to overcome obstacles and thrive in their careers. They are more resilient and confident in their ability to handle the challenges of their line of work, thanks to the support and friendship of other female coaches. Women in the NFL coaching ranks are fostering a strong feeling of unity by using group chats and offering networking opportunities. This creates a welcoming environment where people may openly share ideas, look for wise counsel, and build deep relationships.

The NFL is making a real effort to promote diversity and inclusivity, which is a hope for the future of women coaches, unlike all the previous eras of football. Now, talented individuals have the opportunity to find success even in the NFL, without being excluded because of their gender or orientation, by raising their knowledge and skills.

CHAPTER 6:

Making Their Voices Heard: Women in Announcing

The Rise of Women in Sports Media

The path toward gender equality in sports media has been a difficult and protracted one. Yet, despite the challenges, there has undoubtedly been sluggish and non-linear growth. The examination of women's experiences in sports writing during the last 20 years by Anna Katherine Clemmons illuminates both the advancements and the obstacles that still need to be overcome.

When Clemmons was 26 years old, as a reporter for ESPN The Magazine in 2006, she had direct experience with the difficulties a woman had to enter the field of NFL reporting. Her experience in the Jacksonville Jaguars locker room is evidence of the climate that women in sports journalism have traditionally had to face and try to overcome.

Since then, there have been many positive changes in the sector. More women play significant roles in sports television than in every previous era of sports history. Disparities still exist, however, particularly in sports talk radio, where there were no female celebrities in the top 100 in 2021. The continuous fight for representation is further highlighted by The Institute for Diversity and Ethics in Sport's continued low rating of The Associated Press Sports Editors (APSE) for gender hiring practices.

The turnover rate for women in the news sector after four years is still disproportionately high, even though more women are graduating from journalism schools. This disparity indicates structural problems in the industry that may go beyond sports journalism.

The individual accounts of women who have worked in sports media provide moving insights into these structural problems. Prominent sports journalists Lisa Guerrero and Cari Champion have spoken about their experiences with prejudice and sexism. The toll that the problems of the profession can take on a person are highlighted by Guerrero's account of her time as a Monday Night Football sideline reporter and the harsh criticism that ultimately caused her to quit sports media, as well as Champion's assessment of her job on ESPN's First Take.

Nevertheless, despite these difficulties, there is development and optimism. The story is evolving, if slowly. In addition to being more prevalent in sports media, women are beginning to take formerly male-only roles. The gender discourse in sports media is changing as greater emphasis is placed on the importance of diversity and equality.

Though the road is far from over, the ascent of women in sports media is evidence of their tenacity, willpower, and the slow breaking down of obstacles. It is hoped that as the sports journalism scene develops further, future generations of women journalists will find equal chances, respect, and acknowledgment for their work.

Beth Mowins' Pioneering Career

Elizabeth Mowins was born in 1967 in Syracuse, New York. Since the early 1990s, she has accomplished a career in sports journalism that made her emerge as a leading figure and an example of success and inspiration for women interested in entering this professional field. Mowins has lent her voice as a dynamic play-by-play announcer for several sports, working for top networks such as ESPN, CBS, and the Marquee Sports Network.

Mowins' relationship with sports started at the earliest possible stage of her life, as her father was a high school basketball coach, and she had three brothers who were all into sports and physical exercise. So, she loved sports early on, and as a young girl, she used to play any team sport she could when she was a student at Cicer-North Syracuse High School. She played basketball, softball, and soccer, and later, as a college student at Lafayette College, she played for the varsity basketball team. She was also the captain of the team in two seasons, demonstrating her leadership abilities.

Mowins graduated from Lafayette College in 1989 with a bachelor's degree and then continued her academic studies at the S.I. Newhouse School of Public Communications, obtaining a master's degree in broadcast and digital journalism. Right after her graduation, Mowins was hired as the news and sports director at WXHC-FM Radio in Homer, New York. She was so committed to and successful at her job that three years later, in 1994, she was hired by ESPN for the position of the network's softball coverage's primary voice. Apart from softball, where she covered the Women's College World Series, Mowins has worked as the announcer in a variety of collegiate sports, including volleyball and basketball. Her adaptability to different sports is remarkable and has contributed to establishing her reputation as a leading authority in sports media.

In 2005, Mowins became the second female ESPN college football game caller, establishing herself in the field of sports journalism. Having already accomplished a successful career in a sector where female presence was scarce, Mowins marked an authentic turning point in 2017, when she became the first woman to call an NFL game on national TV, making history. She repeated the same milestone a few years later, in 2021, this time for a basketball game, becoming the first female play-caller on network TV for an NBA game.

These successes were huge for Elizabeth Mowin's professional life, but most importantly, they represent a change in the sports broadcasting industry, which is becoming much more open to women and is leaving behind old prejudices. Opportunities for young women who want to follow the sports broadcaster profession are undoubtedly much greater than they used to be just a few decades ago, and women like Mowins have definitely marked and contributed to this change, showing that gender should not be a limiting factor when a person has the skills, the abilities, and the passion to work in the sports industry.

Kate Scott's Journalist Journey

Kate Scott was born in Fresno in 1983 or 1984, and after spending her childhood in Clovis, California, and graduating from high school in 2001, she continued her education at the University of California, Berkeley, where she discovered a new outlet for her interest in athletics and media. So, she started her path into the world of sports journalism at an early age. Her first job was while she was still at Berkeley, being the "Mic Man" of the University's team, the one who leads cheers for football and basketball games. She was the first woman in this position at Berkeley. She also contributed to ESPN-linked *The Bear Insider* magazine and website. Her time spent in college provided her with a solid groundwork for her future career in sports media, culminating in the awarding of a degree in communications in the year 2005.

The career route that Scott has chosen exemplifies her diverse abilities and dogged perseverance. From the time she began working for Metro Networks, she handled a wide range of tasks, including anything from traffic and news to sports updates across a number of radio stations in the Bay Area. She began by providing coverage of the NBC-owned CSN California network, now called simply NBC California, and then extended her responsibilities to include presenting postgame radio programs and providing sideline coverage for the San Jose Earthquakes team.

Scott is skilled in a variety of sports, including soccer, basketball, softball, and volleyball, in addition to American football, and during her career, she has covered a wide spectrum of events, including calling games for the National Basketball Association, the National Hockey League, NCAA football, and also the top international sports events, i.e., the Olympics and a FIFA World Cup. There were several pioneering events during Scott's career, each of which represented a big step forward for women working in sports journalism. In 2016, Scott made history as the first woman to announce an NFL game on the radio. The next year, in 2017, she made history again as the first woman to announce an American football game for the Pac-12 Network.

Furthermore, on March 8, 2020, in honor of International Women's Day, NBCSN transmitted a National Hockey League game with an all-women's broadcast crew for the first time, and Scott was part of it. In March 2021, she became the first woman to announce a game for the Golden State Warriors and an NBA game on the radio. This achievement further solidified her reputation as a pioneer in the realm of sports broadcasting, which she had already established. Additionally, her voice has been used for the broadcast of international soccer on Fox Sports and CBS Sports. She has also been the preseason television voice for the Seattle Seahawks of the National Football League. Both of these platforms are owned and operated by the same company.

Scott's personal background and the way she was raised are also key factors in her tale, in addition to the professional accomplishments she has achieved. She was elected to the Jewish Sports Hall of Fame of Northern California, having been brought up in the practices and traditions of the Jewish religion. The journey that Scott takes with her wife Nicole and their rescue pit bull, Piper, adds an extra dimension of complexity to her tale and shows the manner in which her personal and professional life smoothly blend together to build her identity.

Scott's legacy can encourage women who aspire to work in sports media since she is the only woman to have called games across such a wide variety of sports, and she is also one of the few voices who have achieved this distinction regardless of gender.

Trailblazers in Sports Media

As in all other topics covered in this book, there are many more women who deserve to be mentioned and who are examples of success and progress in terms of gender equality and inclusivity. A reflection of the larger fight for gender equality in the workplace can be seen in the path that women have taken in this sector, which includes overcoming misconceptions, knocking down obstacles, and establishing new standards. In this section, we'll briefly see the perspectives of six eminent professionals—five women and one man—spanning the last half-century, the obstacles that have been encountered, the advancements that have been accomplished, and the path that lies ahead in the field of sports media.

Christine Brennan: A Perspective From a Pioneering Individual

Christine Brennan began her career with the Miami Herald in 1981 and moved on to the Washington Post in 1984. She attributes her unwavering confidence to the education she received and the supportive professional network she works with. The fact that Brennan was subjected to gender prejudices did not discourage her; rather, it served to strengthen her dedication to excellence and her campaign for equal access in the field of sports reporting. The achievements that she has accomplished and her hopeful vision for the future of women in sports journalism are highlighted by her leadership in the Association of Women in Sports Media and her mentoring of younger women.

Arielle Chambers: A champion in women's sports.

The path that Arielle Chambers took from being a sports fanatic in Raleigh, North Carolina, to becoming a major voice in the media covering women's sports exemplifies the necessity of representation and narrative. Through her work with Bleacher Report's HighlightHer and NBA TV, Chambers has made a concerted effort to close the coverage gap that exists between men's and women's sports in the media. There is substantial progress that has been made but also ongoing difficulties that remain in the way of bringing women's sports more into the mainstream, and Chamber has experienced both conditions. Her career points out the significance of authenticity, mentoring, and community in the process of cultivating a sports media environment that is more encouraging of diversity.

Andrea Kremer: Demonstrating the Capability to Conquer Sexism

Another example of the progression of women's involvement in sports media is Andrea Kremer's illustrious career, which began with her becoming the first female producer at NFL Films and culminated in her breakthrough job at ESPN. On the other hand, Kremer has faced incidences of sexism and pressure from the high expectations that are often placed on women, in the sense that sometimes they have to prove themselves more in order to be accepted. Nevertheless, her rigorous preparation, profound knowledge of the sports she covered, and uncompromising professionalism have gained her success and also blazed the path for other women working in the field.

John Skipper: An Ally's Efforts to Promote Diversity

During his time at ESPN, John Skipper demonstrated the potential effect that can be achieved by leadership that is devoted to diversity and inclusion. His proactive approach to employing a diverse staff and fighting for greater exposure for women's sports demonstrates a knowledge of the impact that the media has in molding the views that society has regarding gender and race. The actions taken by Skipper underlined the significant role that allies play in advancing equality in sports media, highlighting the need to institute rules and processes that are purposefully designed to welcome diversity.

Laura Okmin: Moving From a Competitive to a Collaborative Attitude

During the course of her story, Laura Okmin goes from having to deal with overt sexism to helping to cultivate a network of ladies working in sports journalism. As an example of the transition from considering other women in the sector as rivals to viewing them as partners, her program, named GALvanize, is a successful example. When it comes to overcoming obstacles in the workplace, Okmin's tale serves as a powerful reminder of the significance of support networks, mentoring, and the collective power of women who advocate for each other's success.

Melissa Stark: Displaying Grace and Poise in the Face of Adversity

Melissa Stark's experiences, which range from coping with misinterpreted intentions to addressing open discrimination, are illustrative of the many problems that women in sports journalism encounter. The modest but unmistakable progress toward female equality in sports broadcasting is highlighted by her work with Monday Night Football and Sunday Night Football on NBC. Stark's journey serves as an excellent example of how to strike a balance between perseverance and resilience, showing how professionalism and dedication can successfully demand respect and promote advancement.

Looking to the Future

The six experts that we had a short encounter with all have different backgrounds, but they all take part in and contribute to the continuous changes that the sports journalism industry is experiencing. A more inclusive and fairer atmosphere is getting closer to being achieved inside the industry with each barrier that is broken and old stereotypes that become outdated inside the broader social and cultural evolution. On the other hand, we must not forget that we are in a transition period that is far from complete. There is still work to be done to arrive at a point where gender equality and overcoming exclusion and limitations won't be an issue anymore. Continuous work, lobbying, and allyship are required in order to address the persistent problems of representation, sexism, and the underrepresentation of women's sports in the television and radio media.

The collaborative activity of trailblazers, newcomers, and allies alike will be crucial in crafting a future in which gender will no longer be a determining factor in one's capacity to cover, commentate, or lead in sports media. This will be the case as the industry continues to go through its evolution as it has over the its history so far. The progress that has been made up to this point is not a finish line but rather a light that guides the way toward a sports media ecosystem that is more inclusive and equal.

CHAPTER 7:

Behind the Whistle: Women in Refereeing

—◆—

Progress and Persisting Problems

The development of women's football and their presence in men's football is a major step toward inclusion and gender equality in sports. However, we've already seen that beyond the advancements, professionals and experts in the field agree that American football continues to be a complicated terrain in terms of equality. This is also noticeable in the positions of women referees. On one hand, there has been substantial progress; on the other, there has been persistent discrimination and prejudice.

First, there is an objective factor that has to do with access to the field from the beginning. For women to enter the football world as officials or coaches means they enter a male-dominated industry. Women's presence often continues to be perceived as odd and unnatural, and women who work or want to work in this field will often have to face this problem as parts of society demonstrate a reluctance to accept them in positions previously connected exclusively with men. There can be other obstacles, even of a technical nature, like insufficient facilities for women.

On the other hand, those problems should not end up being used as excuses for lack of skills and effort because this happens sometimes, too. When women want to enter as professionals in men's sports, they must be prepared to face competition and comparison exactly as men do. People who ask for some kind of protection and smooth treatment of women do not help them grow to the level and skills that are needed to become professionals in the gridiron world. Moreover, they don't understand that their attitude is discriminatory in the inverse; that is, it must be equally rejected.

We need to consider and promote competition regardless of gender. Female referees, or, of course, players and coaches, should learn to deal with comparisons as a normal part of assimilating into a common professional sector. The standards of competence and excellence must be exactly the same regardless of gender or race, and people who want to work and have success in the field should be prepared and trained at the necessary level.

Yet, there can be cases where women are unfairly discriminated against only because of their gender or face sexism and other underestimating and offensive behavior. There is often a problematic dynamic between gaining or maintaining professional credibility in the American football field and being feminine at the same time. Apart from humor and perseverance, becoming or appearing more masculine is a coping mechanism that women often use in order to gain respect and become more accepted in the field, bouncing back against sexism in a delicate balancing act. The creative ways in which female football players continue to be passionate and dedicated to the game can be inspiring, but it's evident that having to resort to similar tactics shows the difficulties encountered and the need for more effort in order for football to genuinely become a sport for everyone, regardless of gender.

How to Increase the Representation of Women in Refereeing Roles

It is vital to use a diversified strategy that includes mentoring, training programs, and awareness campaigns to overcome the ongoing gender inequities in football, notably in officiating jobs. The following methods and activities are offered to promote a more inclusive atmosphere and enhance the representation of women in these roles.

Programs That Provide Mentoring

Establishing a peer mentorship program in which experienced women referees assist novices and give the necessary support, direction, and encouragement is an example of peer-to-peer mentoring. This project contributes to the development of self-assurance, the exchange of experiences, and the successful navigation of problems within the profession.

The practice of encouraging male referees who are committed to gender equality to coach female referees may also be useful. This kind of mentoring is known as cross-gender mentoring. It makes the transfer of skills easier and contributes to the modification of views and attitudes among male commissioners.

Initiatives Regarding Training

Training Materials That Are Inclusive: The creation and use of training materials that represent the variety of referees, including the showcasing of successful female referees, has the potential to motivate and educate all referees about the importance of diversity in officiating.

Specialized Training Seminars: Seminars that address specific challenges that women referees experience may provide them with the tools they need to deal with particular obstacles, such as sexism and harassment. These courses should also emphasize leadership and effective negotiating abilities to empower women referees in their jobs.

Training Programs for Women in Refereeing: Courses that are designed exclusively for women may create a comfortable learning atmosphere, encourage more women to attend, and cover themes that are directly relevant to their experiences. While training that is open to both genders is crucial, it is also necessary to provide the courses specifically for women.

Campaigns to Raise Awareness

Launching public awareness campaigns that promote gender equality in sports officiating, challenge misconceptions, and showcase the accomplishments of female referees is an example of a public awareness campaign. By using a variety of media outlets, these campaigns have the potential to reach a large audience and alter the attitudes of the general public.

Working closely with football clubs and teams to teach them about the significance of gender equality in officiating is an example of engagement with clubs and teams. Among them are the encouragement of teams to provide assistance for female referees and the promotion of an atmosphere that is friendly to all officials, regardless of gender.

The practice of regularly acknowledging and praising the achievements of female referees at all levels of the sport is referred to as "recognizing and celebrating successes." Not only does this increase the exposure of female referees, but it also inspires others who are interested in becoming officials.

Incorporating New Policies and Structures

Ensuring that football leagues and organizations have clear regulations in place that provide equal access to refereeing opportunities for women is an important step in implementing equal access policies. This package includes the equitable distribution of matches, equal remuneration, and access to opportunities for development.

The football governing bodies should also implement systems to monitor and enforce compliance with regulations regarding gender equality in order to maintain accountability. This involves establishing goals for the number of women employed in refereeing jobs and consistently evaluating the progress that has been made.

When it comes to overcoming economic hurdles, providing financial support in the form of scholarships or other financial incentives to women who want to seek refereeing credentials may be of great assistance. The provision of this assistance has the potential to make refereeing a more appealing and accessible career choice for women.

Through the implementation of these tactics and actions, the football community has the opportunity to strive toward the creation of an atmosphere that is more inclusive and equal for female referees. While it is likely that change will not occur overnight, continuous work and dedication from all parties involved can dramatically enhance the representation of women in football officiating positions as well as the experiences they have in those roles.

Official Robin DeLorenzo

Robin DeLorenzo stands among the pioneering women who managed to enter into officiating jobs in the NFL. The story of Robin DeLorenzo as an official starts in a classroom where her father, Rich DeLorenzo, taught students who were interested in becoming football referees. Considering that there were no women working in officiating jobs at the time in American football, Robin's decision to enter this sector and study officiating was objectively not just about pursuing her individual passion or career aspiration but also about breaking down boundaries based on gender. Indeed, that was the only way for her to utilize what she was studying professionally. Her path through high school football officiating, where she again worked alongside her father, demonstrated her dedication to becoming the best she could be in the field. It is also, in social terms, the demonstration of the fact that excellence in officiating is not a matter of gender but rather of ability, devotion, and the desire to be good at what you do.

DeLorenzo began in junior college and gradually reached Division I and later the NFL itself. She worked her way through the categories, succeeding throughout the difficult route to becoming a top-tier referee. Her story and professional evolution are not only about her own personal accomplishment but also about the ongoing transformation of the NFL from an exclusively male working environment to a league where it is increasingly being accepted that women can contribute to the game of football.

DeLorenzo's experience in the NFL is inspiring for girls and women who would love to try to become professional referees. She can provide insights into the difficulties and benefits of being a football referee at the highest level as a woman. Wearing the official hat for the first time is strange and challenging for anyone, but it can particularly be challenging for a woman. DeLorenzo's views on the challenges of attaining perfection and trying to make progress and become better as a referee, as well as the significance of mentoring, offer unique insights into the professional attitude of NFL officials.

Furthermore, DeLorenzo's career offers a promising image of the supportive climate that now exists inside the NFL for the encouragement and development of referees regardless of their gender. This gives hope for the future for even better conditions and possibilities of professional development. That's a clarion appeal to all those people who have the desire to go beyond old boundaries in their areas of occupation. DeLorenzo's advice to aspiring female officials to put in the effort and learn from every level of the game can be really helpful.

Maia Chaka: The First Black Woman Referee in the NFL

In 2021, Maia Chaka, a health and physical education teacher, broke a huge glass ceiling for the NFL and professional sports officiating, becoming the first black female referee in the greatest American football league. This momentous accomplishment highlights Chaka's extraordinary personal commitment and skill but also represents a larger step forward for inclusivity and diversity in the NFL and the sports industry.

Before she entered the world of professional American football, Chaka worked at a public school in Virginia Beach and was also a referee of college football, with noteworthy assignments in the Pac-12 Conference and the Conference USA. She has always managed to strike a balance between her love of football and education. Her career at the college level certainly paved the way for her career in the NFL. In 2014, she joined the Officiating Development Program of the NFL. This program is promoted by the league in order to prepare college officials like her who are interested in entering the professional level of football officiating.

With her commitment and determination to become a professional referee, Chaka managed to conclude the program after diligent work and persistence to follow her way to her extraordinary goal: being appointed as an NFL official. That was important not only for her personally but also for her community and other women, as mentioned by the senior vice president of NFL football operations, Troy Vincent, Sr. Since Chaka's tale is being commemorated during Women's History Month, it is even more poignant, highlighting her significance as a pioneer and an encouragement to women who want to enter traditionally male-dominated industries.

Chaka's trailblazing appointment comes at a time when diversity and inclusion among the ranks of the NFL and other major sports leagues have become more important, and similar personal accomplishments are being systematically encouraged and promoted. Her presence on the field as a black woman officiating at the top level of American football challenges the old standards and expectations within the sport. It conveys a strong message that hard effort, ability, and drive are the keys to success and that greatness transcends both racial and gender barriers.

Chaka's position as an NFL official is an important step toward normalizing the presence of women in critical roles on the football field, regardless of the relevance of her ethnic and gender identification. It dispels misconceptions and creates opportunities for future generations of female officials who want to enter the industry themselves. It is hoped that when more women like Chaka overcome these obstacles, their accomplishments will become more commonplace in the athletics world rather than an oddity. So, we can definitely say that Maia Chaka's success in becoming the first black woman selected to join the NFL officiating crew is an accomplishment to celebrate for her and also a story that can inspire young people to follow their aspirations with unwavering drive, forgetting about old boundaries and stereotypes.

Sarah Thomas: Pushing the Limits of What's Possible in NCAA Officiating

Sarah Thomas has established herself as a pioneering figure in the area of National Football League officiating, which is dominated by men. She has broken boundaries and established precedents. Her path from the sidelines of college football to the bright lights of the Super Bowl is a shining example of devotion, resiliency, and an unwavering enthusiasm for the sport of football.

Pascagoula, Mississippi, is the place where Sarah Thomas (née Bailey) was born on September 21, 1973. She spent her childhood surrounded by the world of athletics. In addition to being a great athlete at Pascagoula High School, she created history by earning five letters in softball, which was an accomplishment that had never been accomplished before at the time. She received a basketball scholarship at the University of Mobile due to her remarkable athletic ability, and she went on to succeed academically and be named an all-American. Over the course of three seasons, Thomas amassed impressive stats, and she now ranks sixth in the school's history for on-court accomplishments.

The football field was where Thomas discovered her real calling, although in a different role, despite the fact that she had achieved a great deal of success on the basketball floor. She first performed as a varsity high school official in 1999, laying the groundwork for a career in football officiating that would go on to be remarkable. In the following years, she demonstrated great commitment and abilities, which in 2006 secured her an invitation to the officials' camp from the coordinator of Conference USA, Gerry Austin. Passing with success through the camp process and being appointed as a Conference USA referee, Thomas officiated a college football game in the following year. That was the first time a woman performed as a referee in a major college football game.

In a short amount of time, Thomas demonstrated that she was more than competent in managing the many demands that come with officiating at the college level. In 2009, she was the first woman to oversee a bowl game, and in 2011, she made history once more when she became the first woman to officiate at a Big Ten stadium. Her remarkable communication abilities and her capacity to apply the rules in animated moments gained her the respect and trust of both instructors and players.

In 2015, Thomas's career was elevated to the top level as an American football referee. She was hired by the NFL to work as a full-time official. That wasn't a huge professional success for Thomas alone, but a historic moment for the NFL and American football since that was the first time a woman was hired as a full-time official in the league.

She began her tenure on the show in the role of line judge during the 2015 season, although she has since moved on to the job of down judge. Thomas's pioneering accomplishments were concluded in February 2021, when she made history again by being the first woman official to ever reach the ultimate stage of American football, as she officiated in the Super Bowl game. Her pioneering adventure came to an end with this accomplishment.

In her tenure as an officiant, Thomas has shown professionalism and calm in the face of adversity. Despite suffering a broken wrist from a collision that happened during the game in 2016, she managed to recover and finish the match. Even though she is navigating the intricacies of being a pioneer in her area, she has maintained her unshakeable devotion to quality and justice.

During his time away from the field, Thomas has a successful personal life. She and her husband, Brian Thomas, together with their three children, make their home in Brandon, Mississippi. She worked as a pharmaceutical agent prior to becoming a referee, which exemplifies her adaptability and dedication to the interests she has pursued.

It is impossible to overestimate the influence that Sarah Thomas has had on the officiating of the National Football League and the wider world of sports. It is not only that she has torn down boundaries between the sexes, but she has also motivated a great number of women and girls to follow their aspirations in sports, regardless of the challenges they may face. Thomas is a real pioneer and an icon in the history of the NFL because her narrative is one of tenacity, greatness, and the unrelenting pursuit of one's interests without exception.

CHAPTER 8:

Future Prospects for Women in American Football

Women's Sports Evolution

The world of sports, and especially women's sports, is currently experiencing a phase of change and development. Long-standing discrepancies in coverage, financing, and support for female athletes are fading away as society and the economy move on, and many more possibilities open in relation to past eras. It is essential to look deeper into the shifting environment and acknowledge the efforts that were made to overcome older obstacles and open the path toward empowerment and equality.

Nothing can be done without money. So, the rising financial investment and media attention are necessary for any kind of improvement in women's sports. There's a deliberate attempt to help financially so more women can have the chance to be involved in sports that have traditionally been dominated by men. "Grow the Game" is a project that gives grassroots international football clubs an extra three million pounds in funding, and it's one example of this new trend. This trend does not only exist on football fields. On the contrary, it is widespread throughout several sports, and in some cases, such as rugby, it has had impressive results, as the strategies followed and the partnerships made boosted the number of women players at high levels.

Moreover, the Union of European Football Associations (UEFA) has committed to raising financing for women's international football by a robust 50%, and FIFA (the International Association Football Federation) has planned in 2018 to raise the number of women who play football by 100% by 2026. These are very important examples of the shifting views on women's sports in fields previously thought of as exclusively male since these are the two greatest organizations of the most followed sports internationally. American football should keep in mind these attempts made in the world of soccer as it proceeds with its own strategies and policies for the development of female participation in the sport. These kinds of activities are essential to the process of establishing more prominent female role models in the sporting world, which in turn encourages the next generation of young girls to pursue careers in athletics.

A Greater Number of People Participating Has a Ripple Effect

The rise of female athletes has had a considerable impact beyond the field of play. Girls who played sports in their final year of high school were more likely to do well academically and had a decreased incidence of unintended pregnancy. The psychological and physiological advantages of participating in sports are highlighted by the fact that female athletes have greater levels of confidence, self-esteem, and a more favorable body image.

What's crucial as professional athletes, besides providing entertainment, is to provide young people with role models that can encourage and inspire them to enter the world of sports and physical exercise, which is very beneficial for their body, mind, and spirit health and well-being.

Then, the more people participate in sports, the more others find it appealing and exciting to participate as well. Like in many other things and fields, there is a ripple effect.

Now, it's obvious that the more women are into sports, the more girls will tend to follow their example. That's why it's important to find ways to promote women's sports. Women's rugby and hockey, or the growth of women's soccer internationally, are excellent examples of how focused investments and strategic planning can boost women's sports and change their whole setting, even in a brief period.

Women's College Athletics As a Reflection of Society

Society has moved toward recognizing and appreciating the contributions that women athletes make, as seen by initiatives such as the #whatif campaign and the high attendance of supporters at some women's sporting opportunities. This is a reflection of the larger cultural movement toward gender equality and the breakdown of outdated preconceptions that women in sports have encountered in past times.

However, there are also still obstacles to overcome, as there are significant disparities between men and women in terms of financing, professional opportunities, and media attention in sports. Those disparities highlight the need for lobbying and actions to enhance women's presence in leadership roles in sports and encourage gender diversity in all facets of sports.

On the other side, it is necessary to also make an observation that often activists, politicians, and journalists do not make because it's not so easy and pleasant as to say that everything should be perfect, and that is that promoting women's sports cannot be imposed by force or because activists and politicians decide it. Women's sports have to become more attractive and appealing to people and fans, and those who work in the field should actively search for ways that would make the product more appealing. Often, people who talk about equality and diversity forget about this practical part, which, in reality, is the most important of all. That's why we tried to present some ideas followed by international organizations and other sports that maybe could offer some examples for American football, too. Below, we add reflections in that direction and thoughts on how technology can help women's sports and, in particular, women's football.

A Glance Into the Future: The Prospects for Women's Athletics

Rising financial investments, increased exposure, and cultural acceptance of the importance of female athleticism make the future of women's sports bright. This is because women's sports are becoming more visible. As more teenage girls look up to professional female athletes as role models, the dreams of pursuing a career in sports are becoming much more attainable than in previous decades.

It is a credit to the tenacity and resolve of female athletes and campaigners who have challenged the status quo that the progress of women's sports has occurred. Despite the fact that there is still a lot of work to be done, the progress that has been achieved in women's sports provides an encouraging peek into a future in which gender will no longer be a limiting factor in athletic possibilities or accomplishments.

Embracing Technological Advancements to Enhance American Football's Future

So, let's talk about current technological advancements and innovations and how they could help women's football grow. Not only are technical developments causing the game to change, but they are also causing it to undergo a revolution in the world of American football, which is undergoing rapid change. These top ten new technologies are at the vanguard of the sport's future, with the potential to increase player safety and performance as well as revolutionize the experience that fans have with the sport.

Technology That Can Be Worn for Tracking by GPS and Monitoring User Performance

Wearable gadgets have become an integral component in the sport of football because they provide real-time insights into players' performance metrics and health conditions. The incorporation of GPS tracking devices into clothes allows for the collection of crucial data, such as speed, distance traveled, and heart rate, which enables the development of individualized training and injury prevention interventions.

The Use of Impact Sensors and Intelligent Helmets

As a means of addressing the significant problem of head injuries, smart helmets fitted with impact sensors provide very useful information on the forces applied during collisions. This technology makes the rapid identification and treatment of concussions easier while player safety is prioritized.

Instruction Based on Virtual Reality

Virtual reality (VR) technology provides players with a novel and risk-free approach to perfecting their abilities through realistic and engaging simulations of gaming settings. This forward-thinking training improves the ability to make decisions and the cognitive capabilities essential for accomplishing success on the field.

Advanced Video-Analytics

Modern video analytics uses computer vision and machine learning to provide in-depth player performance evaluations and thorough game strategy analysis. This data-driven information can help make coaching choices and strategic planning more accurate.

Artificial Turf of the Next Generation

Today's artificial turf technologies are more accurate than ever before in their ability to imitate real grass. This has resulted in a considerable reduction in the likelihood of injuries occurring, as well as environmental advantages, such as less water use and the integration of recyclable materials.

IoT (Internet of Things) and Smart Stadiums

The Internet of Things is revolutionizing the fan experience through linked stadiums that provide real-time information to fans' mobile devices. This information includes information on seats, catering, and other things. In addition to enhancing stadium operations, the Internet of Things also aims to lessen its environmental impact.

Authentication Based on Biometrics

Player identification and access control are achieved by the use of biometric authentication technologies, such as facial recognition and fingerprint scanning. By enhancing internal security protocols, these technologies safeguard athletes and uphold the integrity of the sport.

Camera Systems That Are Robotic

Robotic camera systems improve game broadcasts and fans' watching experiences by providing unique viewpoints and views. Thanks to their adaptability and accuracy in recording dynamic play activity, new avenues may be explored for content development and analysis.

Innovative Methods for the Prevention and Treatment of Injuries

Wearable sensors are an instrument that can enhance injury prevention and guarantee safe recovery for injured players. Another essential element is the use of data analytics in the creation of tailored rehabilitation programs.

Monitoring of the Health and Wellness of the Players

A comprehensive monitoring of players' sleep patterns, food intake, and stress levels via the use of technology enables holistic approaches to performance improvement. This highlights the significance of off-field well-being in the process of reaching greatness on the field.

A new era for the competitive sport of American football begins with the integration of these recently created technologies. Through its emphasis on innovations that improve player safety, performance, and engagement, football is setting the standard for how sports may innovate and evolve. New technologies create new and broader possibilities, and history teaches us that those who oppose them and do not embrace them have nothing to gain in the long run. Sports, and American football in particular, have a lot to gain by embracing the new technologies, and that would be crucial for the sport to continue to grow and have success and popularity in the future, as it has always had during the history of American and international sports. The success of American football has been attributed to its ability to adjust to changing circumstances and always move in the direction of new ideas; the terrain is dynamic and ever-changing.

How Technology Relates to Women's American Football

The rapid technological progress gives hope for a brighter future for female American football players, along with the improvement in the popularity of women's sports in general. The introduction of new technology brings a transformation of the game, which becomes safer and more accessible for female players thanks to the new features and possibilities. For instance, smart helmets and impact sensors are being used to improve the detection and measurement of head hits, which has resulted in a considerable improvement in player safety and the avoidance of concussion damage. This technical innovation is essential for the future of the sport since it puts an end to the long-standing problem of head injuries and creates a more secure playing environment for all players, including female athletes.

Virtual reality is another innovation that can affect the future of football since players can use it to train in artificial game-like conditions. Indeed, VR training provides players with the opportunity to practice in a realistic, three-dimensional environment via the use of simulation-based training, just like the fighter pilots and astronauts in the simulators have done for decades. Advances in technology now offer similar opportunities in sports and entertainment. This incredible technology, which only a few years ago would have looked like science fiction, gives female players the chance to improve their agility and cultivate their talent, acquiring new moves without the physical hazards that can be, and indeed, often are, connected with regular practice. This technology is especially advantageous for female athletes. The use of virtual reality training helps enhance decision-making and response speed, both of which are vital for success in the field.

The utilization of powerful video analytics, which is driven by computer vision and machine learning, is causing a remarkable transformation in the manner in which coaches and analysts comprehend and analyze the game. The use of this technology makes it possible to conduct a more in-depth analysis of player performance and game plans. This may be of particular use to women's teams, as it can provide insights that enable more efficient training and growth.

The artificial turf of the next generation is enhancing player safety by imitating the feel of real grass. This might allow more women to engage in football by minimizing the danger of injuries that are connected to older artificial turf systems. In addition to this, these innovative surfaces have positive effects on the environment, which are in line with wider social movements toward sustainability.

These technical developments, together with greater media attention and financing, are paving the way for a more inclusive and egalitarian future in the sport of women's football, which is continuing to expand at a rapid pace. Increasingly, the infrastructure for women's football is being strengthened as a result of the formation of professional leagues such as the Women's Football Alliance and the Women's National

Football Conference, as well as measures to assist female football at the high school and university levels.

In the context of American football, these trends together point to a bright future for women in the sport. Improvements in safety, training, and support systems might result in increased participation rates and possibilities for women at all levels of the sport.

"The Gender Bowl"

Technological progress sounds promising and potentially useful for women's sports and in particular football, but returning to the present time, and in fact, some years in the past, we will have to land on a social reality that still seems to need improvement in terms of its receptiveness to women's American football and women in football.

An academic article by Jacqueline McDowell and Spencer Schaffner, published in 2011, discusses the gender dynamics and stereotypes that are prevalent in American football, with a special emphasis placed on the active involvement of women in the sport, highlighting the debate and conflict that emerges when women participate in a sport that is often associated with men. The article examines a reality television show called "The Gender Bowl," where there was a football game between men and women, aiming to investigate the reactions to the participation of women in the sport, which is traditionally more associated with men, and how the conventional masculine identity and discourse are challenged by that. The results showed how conservative, conflictual, and egalitarian gender discourses interact in a complicated way.

It became clear that the men who participated in the reality program wanted to maintain the established gender dynamics and roles of football, portraying the sport as a male endeavor. They made statements that doubted the women's understanding of the game and their physical preparedness for it. Their views implied that women are intrinsically and genetically unsuited to meet the demands of a hard, rough-and-tumble game like football. Moreover, these views perpetuate the stereotype of the weak woman who needs to be protected. The assertion of masculine supremacy in the sport was often accompanied by the use of insults and language that was derogatory. As an example, they stated that women did not possess the intellectual capability to comprehend football and that their physical nature rendered them unsuitable for the game owing to their lack of physical ability. The intention of these comments was to prevent women from participating in football by portraying the sport as fundamentally inaccessible to them.

Furthermore, the article emphasizes the ways in which gender preconceptions impacted people's opinions of women's involvement in football. In order to argue against women's participation in the sport, traditional notions of femininity, such as being elegant and non-aggressive, were utilized as arguments. A few of the group voiced the opinion that women should be confined to their traditional duties of being nursed and protected rather than playing football.

The study pointed out the vocabulary used by male and female players, underlining some characteristic differences in the way men and women addressed each other. Men often used disparaging names such as "girls" to belittle female players, like saying that football is a men's game. On the other hand, women referred to themselves as "ladies," which can be seen as an indication of a desire for equal treatment and respect in the sport.

A key discovery was that talks between the women players in the reality show indeed had egalitarian elements, as they asserted their physical capability and right to equal involvement. However, the study also shows that women claimed their equal involvement and opposed contrary preconceptions more than challenging the masculine nature of the sport by employing terminology that is often associated with men themselves, including insults.

In general, the research findings indicate that there is a tension and contrast between conventional gender standards in football and the quest for equality in the sport. Women tried to fight these conventions by expressing their right to play as equals on the field, while men attempted to preserve the status of male superiority and supremacy in football. Yet, men acknowledged the women's efforts, and women implicitly acknowledged there was a masculine drive to the sport in the sense that it was tough and physical.

The Quest for Equality in American Football

Women have made considerable progress in American football over the course of the years. This progression is demonstrated by personalities such as Sam Gordon, whose extraordinary skill and campaigning have brought attention to the potential and enthusiasm of female players in the sport of football. Not only did Gordon's viral popularity as a young football prodigy defy preconceptions, but it also sparked a movement for the creation of new chances in the sport that are accessible to people of many different backgrounds. Pioneering individuals such as Gordon are working to challenge the paternalistic attitudes that have traditionally marginalized women's football.

These attitudes have been a barrier to progress. In order to address the significant disparity in the number of possibilities for involvement that exists between boys and girls, Gordon has established the Utah Girls Tackle Football League, which serves as an essential platform for young girls to participate in football for the first time. The goal of this effort is not only to cultivate talent; rather, it is to challenge the structural restrictions that have prevented females from playing football at the same level as boys.

Beyond youth leagues, there is a broad range of competition for recognition. Despite the fact that women are demonstrating their ability on the field, there are still few opportunities for them to play professionally.

As the sport of football continues to develop, the role of advocates and allies in confronting outmoded standards and opening opportunities for female players will develop into an increasingly important one. The idea of a football world that is more egalitarian and inclusive is within reach, and it is being propelled by the devotion and passion of those individuals who refuse to accept the present status quo. It is a monument to the resiliency and drive of women who dare to dream big and fight hard for their place on the field, and the progress that has been accomplished up to this point serves as a foundation for the continuous path toward equality in sports.

The Impact of Athletics on Female Academic Achievement

Participation in sports and athletic activities helps not only the body but also the mind and the soul. We can find extensive and clear evidence for that by examining the academic and educational achievements, in particular, of female high school students. Indeed, the participation of young women in interscholastic sports throughout their high school years not only contributes to the improvement of their physical well-being but also drives them toward better academic performance and superior educational results. Girls who engage in sports and physical exercise tend to have better results and enter the academic world with more consistency. Additionally, compared to their counterparts who did not engage in athletics, they had a higher likelihood of finishing college after high school.

Self-control, time-management, and teamwork skills acquired on the field translate into enhanced performance in the classroom. Sports participation appears to benefit males more than females in mathematics; the opposite is true for science and vocabulary (Veliz, P. et al., 2014). This multifaceted approach sheds light on the intricate relationship that exists between gender, academic fields, and athletics, and it suggests that involvement in sports may bring distinct cognitive advantages across a variety of topics.

The association between engagement in sports and academic success is further shown by attendance figures, which provide further evidence. Research carried out in the states of Minnesota and North Carolina discovered that high school athletes had a lower rate of absences than students who did not participate in athletics (Women's Sports Foundation, 2020). There is a strong possibility that the greater school attendance of athletes is a contributing factor to their improved academic performance and grade point averages.

In the state of Kansas, female high school athletes reported having grade point averages that were much higher than those of non-athletes. According to Lumpkin and Favor (2012), a greater proportion of female athletes reported having a grade point average of three or higher, and the disparity was even more obvious when the overall grade point average was three and a half or higher. The statistical data presented here implies that the advantages of participating in sports go beyond the realm of physical health and extend into the realm of academic achievement.

The same research found that female athletes graduated from high school at a rate that was eight percent higher than that of female non-athletes and that they were much less likely to drop out of high school when compared to their peers who did not participate in athletics. This highlights the long-term effect. It would seem from this that involvement in sports is of utmost importance in maintaining the interest and retention of female students in the educational system.

According to data released by the NCAA in 2018, female athletes graduated at greater rates than the general undergraduate population. However, there were significant discrepancies in the rates of graduation across different racial groups. Women of white, black, and Hispanic/Latino descent who participated in athletics all had graduation rates that were greater than those of their peers in the general student population. It is clear from this that engagement in sports has a significant influence on increasing educational achievement across a wide range of demographic areas.

The findings provide a strong picture of the positive effect that participation in high school athletics has on the academic performance of female students. Sport provides young women with an organized route to not only test and develop their physical talents but also to increase their intellectual and scholastic possibilities. This is accomplished by cultivating an atmosphere that is disciplined and favorable to learning and growth. Youth sports provide this opportunity. It is clear that the values taught in the field, such as perseverance, collaboration, and resilience, are similar to those that are required to thrive academically. This highlights the significance of athletics as an essential component of the scholastic growth and success of females.

Overcoming the Obstacles: Increasing the Number of Women Participating in Sports

Research and studies have shown a complex web of obstacles that prevent women from participating in sports. These obstacles include financial limits, access concerns, social dynamics, and structural disadvantages (UN Women, 2020).

The availability of financial resources is a significant obstacle that prevents girls and women in the United States from participating in sports. The pay-for-play system, which came into existence as a result of schools redirecting funding from extracurricular activities, including sports programs, to other areas owing to increasing budgetary constraints, has had a disproportionately negative influence on the availability of sports for female students. There are many people who are unable to participate in sports because of the high cost of participation, which includes school sports fees, the costs connected with community activities, and the costs of travel teams. This financial strain is even more obvious for families who are supporting their daughters' participation in sports, where the expenditures might include membership fees, equipment, and coaching.

Despite the fact that school budgets are either remaining the same or dropping, fees for community-based sports are increasing. Furthermore, 42% of families with low incomes cited the cost of participation as the primary obstacle that prevents their children from participating in sports. There is a significant discrepancy in the number of people who participate in sports across different socioeconomic categories, which highlights the need for more equitable financing structures and scholarship possibilities to close the gap.

Girls and women face sociological and cultural challenges in addition to financial restrictions. These barriers include a lack of good role models, inadequate media coverage and attendance at women's sports events, and a general impression of athletics as a sector that is dominated by men.

According to a poll covering the entire United States, 60% of respondents think that girls do not have equal chances to participate in sports, and only 43% thought they were aware of how to assist girls' active engagement with sports. It is evident that the majority in the United States believe that schools and colleges provide greater support for boys' and men's sports programs than they do for girls' and women's sports programs.

This finding is further exacerbated by the fact that female athletes are not given sufficient attention in the media. The lack of support and recognition that exists between male and female athletes is a barrier to the expansion of female participation in sports. This highlights the significance of providing female athletes with equal chances and increasing their exposure.

The difference between minority groups and majority groups in terms of involvement in sports is another key cause for worry. When compared to majority groups, minority groups often have fewer resources and opportunities available to them. This disparity is most noticeable in the participation rates of American girls.

Furthermore, there is an evident and significant connection between girls' desire and facility to engage in sports activities and the quality of the social and economic environments where they live. This connection is even more evident and considerable when it comes to the safety of their neighborhoods. Girls who live in places where there is a high rate of criminality are less likely to participate in sports and physical exercise. This finding highlights the need to provide communal places that are both safe and easily accessible for all children to play and be active.

Concentrated efforts will be needed from every sector of society in order to break down these obstacles. The provision of financial assistance programs, scholarships, and legislative changes that are targeted at making sports more accessible and inexpensive may be of critical importance in the process of providing support for female athletes. In addition, the promotion of good role models, the enhancement of the visibility of female athletes, and the establishment of safe settings for participation in sports are all essential steps toward attaining gender equality in the competition of sports.

The collaborative effort toward inclusiveness, equal opportunity, and support for girls and women in sports continues to be an essential undertaking for the development of a more equitable and diversified athletic scene. This is especially true as the United States continues to negotiate these obstacles.

The Increasing Participation of Women in Athletics: A Step Towards Equality and Empowerment

In recent years, the discrepancy between men's and women's participation and interest in sports has diminished considerably, and that's a significant change with respect to previous eras. This progress would not be possible without the perseverance and tenacity of sportswomen who, for decades, have been participating in sports in spite of gender stereotypes and limitations. Their stance contributed a lot to altering the perceptions and expectations in the world of sports.

What the Pioneers Left Behind and the Current Surge in Demand

The history of women in sports has been shaped by significant moments and legendary personalities who have bucked the odds all throughout their careers. As a symbol of resistance against gender limitations in athletics, Katherine Switzer's historic race in the 1967 Boston Marathon, which she had completed while wearing bib number 261, is still remembered today. Switzer's involvement, in spite of the fact that she was explicitly opposed to it, paved the way for millions of women to follow in her footsteps. She transformed the marathon running competition, which had previously been controlled by males, into a worldwide stage where female athletes may demonstrate their determination and strength.

In the years that followed, the number of women who participate in sports has considerably increased. This tendency has been strongly affected by the modifications that were implemented in schools throughout the 1970s. As a result of their inspiration from her story, successors to Switzer's legacy, such as Yelena Isinbayeva, Serena Williams, Simone Biles, and about half of the world's female population, are now participating in some type of physical activity.

The Closing of the Gender Gap

This growth in participation is mirrored in the changing dynamics of the Olympic Games, where women have participated in all categories of sports since 2012. This is a significant milestone that highlights the progress that has been made toward gender equality in the athletic arena. Women's sports have been further driven into the limelight as a result of the impact of mass media, which has challenged long-standing preconceptions and opened up new chances for female athletes.

The Obstacles and the Path That Lies Ahead

There are still substantial barriers that women in sports must overcome, notwithstanding the progress that has been made. The complete achievement of gender equality in athletics is hampered by the continued existence of cultural norms, social expectations, and discrepancies in resources and support. To provide just one example, girls who come from immigrant households or who belong to minority populations sometimes face extra layers of hurdles. These problems might range from financial limits to a lack of access to facilities and coaching.

Not only that, but the struggle against long-standing preconceptions and the need for recognition extend beyond the confines of the playing field. Female athletes aspire for equal treatment and representation, not just in terms of participation but also in terms of media attention, financial assistance, and support from society.

Inspiring and Enhancing the Next Generation

In order to maintain the momentum toward gender equality in sports, it is essential to implement programs that stimulate involvement in sports beginning at a young age, ensure equal access to resources and coaching, and fight detrimental gender stereotypes.

Because it advocates the larger concepts of equality, empowerment, and inclusion, the emergence of women in sports is not simply a success for athletes; it is also a victory for society worldwide. As we look to the future, the legacy of pioneers such as Katherine Switzer and the accomplishments of modern champions will undoubtedly motivate generations of women to follow their athletic dreams, significantly reducing the gender gap and transforming the landscape of sports.

UN Women Promotes Equality and Women's Sports

The Beijing Platform for Action of the United Nations Women, signed by 189 countries in 1995, was the most ambitious and comprehensive plan ever created to achieve gender equality and represents a milestone in this cultural process. Walking into the 2020s, the UN Women promoted the Generation Equality initiative, aiming to bring fresh air and new momentum for the advancement of gender equality and the Beijing Platform for Action goals.

In recent times, the potential importance of sports in the whole process has become increasingly clear, and it's widely accepted that sports have a key role to play as they are crucial for girls' empowerment. Sports, in general, can offer examples and values and prepare young people to be collaborative, get over adversities, and persevere to achieve goals. Moreover, sports are beneficial because they transcend borders and cultural, political, and religious differences and create a sense of commonality and unity more easily than most other activities.

As the report of the above-mentioned UN initiative points out, sports activities are beneficial to physical health, education, self-esteem, and leadership abilities. For women, they help by challenging and overcoming old gender stereotypes—like the ones that have surrounded women's football for a long time in history.

Sports organizations have made serious efforts to promote gender equality in the last few years. Development programs for girls and women are much more common, and the number of women in key positions in the sports industry has increased substantially. So have the resources allocated for the growth of women's sports. Furthermore, media coverage has excluded any type of prejudice relative to gender.

On the other hand, the difficulties of the process of gender equality are not entirely over. Negative stereotypes often persist, just like gender-based violence. For that reason, the United Women's initiative Sport for Generation Equality invites the sports community worldwide to fully implement the concept of equality since, in many cases, it remains an ideal more than an experienced reality. Governments, sports federations, agencies, and the media participate in the project, and they are committed to providing equal opportunity for girls to participate in sports activities, encouraging women's leadership, and also addressing gender-based violence. For all that, money is needed, so they are committed to raising investment and funding for women's sports.

UN Women and the Sport for Generation Equality Initiative invite the entire sports community and any kind of sports-related institution to work together for a common goal for the first time, exchanging practices and learning from one another. The number of participants has steadily increased in these years, including essential actors such as the International Olympic Committee.

An invitation to inquire about being a member of the Sport for Generation Equality Initiative is extended to those who are enthusiastic about making a contribution to this worldwide endeavor and bringing about gender equality in and through the realm of sports. The power of sports as a catalyst for change, unity, and empowerment is being celebrated via this project, which not only marks a new chapter in the battle for gender equality but also celebrates the power of physical activity.

CHAPTER 9:

Impact of Trailblazing Women on American Football

—◆—

More Women in Key Jobs in the NFL

In recent years, inside the NFL, there has been growing acceptance and acknowledgment of women's skills, which is reflected in a trend of increasing the number of women who work in key jobs for the league. This trend defies long-standing gender conventions from older times and deeply modifies the topography of the most popular sport in the United States. This development is a significant step toward inclusiveness and diversity and accompanies wider cultural shifts that are taking place in the same direction.

A characteristic example of this trend is Catherine Raiche's career. She began working as a college scout, and thanks to her successful presence, she became the assistant general manager and vice president of football operations for the Cleveland Browns. Having achieved the highest-ranking female executive position in the league's history, Raiche is objectively an example of overcoming the exclusive association of men with positions of that height in the sports industry.

As for the 2023 NFL season, the number of women who worked full-time coaching or football operations jobs has reached an impressive 223 (Sports Business Journal, 2023). This marked a significant increase from the 2022 season and an astounding 141% increase since the year 2020. The substantial improvement that has been made highlights the efforts that have been made to include women in all aspects of the NFL, be they coaching staff jobs, referee crews, front offices, and personnel departments. The league recognizes the need for additional growth despite these accomplishments since women continue to fall behind in terms of equal representation. Moreover, the NFL has to deal with charges that vary from toxic workplace conditions, which, of course, can regard men and women alike, to all-out gender discrimination.

The dedication of the NFL to promoting gender equality is made clear by efforts such as the NFL Women's Forum, which is led by Sam Rapoport, who is the Senior Director of Diversity, Equity, and Inclusion for the league. In an effort to address the historically low number of chances available to women in football, the forum intends to facilitate connections between female applicants and clubs. An increasing number of people are participating in the forum, which is a reflection of a league-wide embrace of gender diversity. Rapoport's goal of a more inclusive NFL is gradually becoming a reality.

The inclusion of women in key roles within the NFL can not only bring about a balance that was lacking in the past, but it could also enhance the sport by reflecting the variety that exists in society, making it more attractive and accessible to parts of the society that considered it alien to them. It is starting to challenge and alter the dynamics of the league, making it a more inclusive environment that prioritizes skill and devotion above gender. This is because the inclusion of women in different positions is beginning to challenge and change the dynamics of the league.

On the other hand, the struggle to achieve gender equality in the NFL is not without its obstacles. The complicated difficulties that are now being faced by the league are brought to light by the controversy that has surrounded the signing of quarterback Deshaun Watson by the Browns, despite allegations of sexual misconduct against Watson. These occurrences highlight the need to maintain a state of constant monitoring and taking action in order to cultivate an atmosphere that is courteous and equal for all members of the NFL community.

The NFL is entering a period of profound change, as seen by the increasing number of women who are assuming key positions within the organization. However, despite the fact that tremendous progress has been achieved in the direction of gender equality, the path is not yet complete. The dedication of the NFL to cultivating an atmosphere that is diverse and inclusive creates the possibility of a future in which talent, regardless of gender, is acknowledged and appreciated, thereby paving the way for a league that is more equal and dynamic.

Women NFL Owners

We can also trace the trend at the highest level of occupation with the NFL, which is being the owner of a franchise. Below, we'll briefly discuss three female owners of NFL teams: Amy Adams Strunk, owner of the Tennessee Giants; Sheila Ford Hamp, owner of the Detroit Lions; and Carlie Irsay-Gordon, co-owner and vice chair of the Indianapolis Colts.

Amy Adams Strunk

Amy Adams Strunk was born on September 29, 1955. Her family was wealthy and comprised oil entrepreneurs and business executives, and her father, Bud Adams, among other businesses, owned the Tennessee Giants of the NFL. Strunk studied at the University of Texas in Austin, where she got a degree in history, and she has always worked for her family businesses, such as the Bud Adams Ranches, Inc. and the Little River Oil and Gas Company. But most importantly, when her father died, Strunk inherited a third of the Tennessee Titans. Another third went to her sister, and another third to her brother's widow and two sons.

Initially, the controlling owner was Strunk's sister, Susie Adams Smith, with her husband in the position of the chairman of the team. However, their management was probably problematic, and a couple of years later, the family appointed Strunk as the controlling owner. Along with her nephew, S. Adams IV, Strunk hired Steven Underwood as president and CEO of the organization, a business partner of the family for years. They also hired Jon Robinson as the team's general manager. Strunk and her nephew have been very active, and they have a good relationship and contact with fans and people in Nashville, as well as with the shareholders. They accept feedback from them and promote the team in the area, something Strunk's father did not do, being much more distant and disinterested in the team.

Thanks to her successful leadership, the NFL's Hall of Fame committee appointed her a member in 2016. Moreover, the Pro Football Hall of Fame elected her to the Board of Trustees. Another accolade for Strunk's running of the Titans was the NFL doing the league's draft in Nashville, Tennessee's capital, in 2019. For that success, which was considered an honor for the city, the Tennessee Sports Hall of Fame gave her the 2019 Tennessean of the Year award.

In December 2020, Strunk's share of the Titans became even bigger, reaching 50%, as her sister sold her share to KSA Industries, which belongs to the family. That meant the team would be owned by Strunk and her nephews, with her always as the controlling owner.

Sheila Ford Hamp

Sheila Ford Hamp was born on October 31, 1951. She is married to Steve Hamp, and they have three children. Hamp's parents were William Clay Ford, grandson of Henry Ford, and Martha Firestone Ford, whose family owns the Firestone Tire and Rubber Company. Hamp studied at Yale University, among the first women to study there, and got a degree in 1973. Then, she continued her studies at Boston University, where she earned a master's in teaching and early childhood education. She had been interested in sports since she was a student, and she played competitive tennis in high school when she won a state championship in Michigan. She further played competitive tennis during her college years at Yale.

The Fords have owned the Detroit Lions since 1957 without much success. In fact, the Lions are sadly one of the worst teams in the NFL during this historical period, as they are one of the four franchises that have never reached the Super Bowl. Nevertheless, it seems that something is beginning to change under Hamp's leadership, as the team in January 2024 reached only for the second time the National Football Conference's championship game, the first being in 1991, and they came close to qualifying for the Super Bowl, losing to the San Francisco 49ers only by 34-31.

Hamp has been occupied with the Lions since 2014 when her mother took control of the organization as the controlling owner and chairman. On June 23, 2020, Hamp became the controlling owner and chairman; for the first time ever, an NFL organization's ownership passed from one woman to another woman. Right away, Hamp showed she meant business, and she had higher ambitions and standards for the team instead of its decades-long weakness and insignificance; on November 28, she fired head coach Matt Patricia and general manager Bob Quinn, considering them accountable for the bad start in the season. Then, she hired Dan Campell as the new coach and Bran Holmes as general manager. The improvement of the team in the last seasons made her decision look like a genius stroke. Coach Campbell said Hamp is unique, and the three of them collaborate excellently to implement her vision of the Lions becoming a top team.

Carlie Isray-Gordon

Carlie Irsay-Gordon has worked for the Indianapolis Colts since 2004. Her grandfather, Robert Irsay, had been the owner of the organization since 1972, and then it was passed on to her father, Jim Irsay. Irsay-Gordon, who's married to Zach Gordon and has three children with him, studied geoscience and religious studies at Skidmore College and then began a PhD in clinical psychology at Argosy University, although she did not complete the program. Her interest in sports is also shown by the fact she did competitive riding in her college years. Her horse had the funny name London Times.

Isray-Gordon has been the vice president of the Colts since 2008, and she has represented the organization at meetings with other owners since 2004. In 2012, Jim Irsay stated that the franchise would pass entirely to his daughters. Two years later, he was arrested for drug use and entered rehabilitation, with Isray-Gordon being named chair of the Colts. Although her father remains the owner and CEO of the team to this day, Isray-Gordon's influence is essential. Reportedly, in January

2023, she was heavily involved in Colts interviews for hiring a new coach since the beginning, even before her father.

In 2015, the Indianapolis Business Journal selected Isray-Gordon among its list of "Forty Under 40" entrepreneurs, and one year later, she became a member of the NFL Digital Media Committee. In 2024, she is a member of the Media Owned and Operated Committee of the league, which supervises the function of the official website of the NFL and of the NFL Network. Another role Isray-Gordon currently has in the NFL is participating in the Security and Fan Control Committee of the league and being a member of the board of Player Care Foundation, which is a foundation created by the NFL to offer social assistance and services to former players of the league.

As co-owner of the Indianapolis Colts with her sister Karen, Isray-Gordon supports an initiative on mental health called "Kicking the Stigma," which started in May 2021. To achieve the best possible impact, they focused the franchise's charity resources exclusively on this program.

The NFL's Drive for Women's Inclusion

The important shift that is now taking place in the dynamic world of the NFL, ushering in a new age of inclusiveness and diversity in a sport that was previously male dominated, is being spearheaded by visionaries such as Samantha Rapoport, Senior Director of Diversity, Equity, and Inclusion for the NFL, and backed by personalities such as Catherine Raiche, player for the Cleveland Browns, and Dee Haslam, co-owner of the same team.

An important turning point in the history of the NFL occurred in 2017 when the NFL Women's Forum was established. This forum was established by Sam Rapoport with the intention of bringing together female candidates and teams in order to solve the apparent lack of women in positions of authority within football operations, such as coaching, scouting, and other functions. Rapoport's effort, which was driven by her personal and professional enthusiasm for football, aimed to eliminate the obstacles that prohibit women from pursuing professions in the sport that they love.

The Women's Forum has had a significant influence. Since its humble beginnings, the forum has expanded to include all 32 NFL teams, and the degree of involvement has reached the point where there is only room for standing players. The league's dedication to achieving gender equality and removing hurdles that have persisted for a long time is reflected in the exponential expansion of the player pool.

When women are allowed to play in the NFL, it is not only about redressing gender disparities; it is also about improving the sport itself. It has been seen by general managers that the incorporation of women into scouting operations has resulted in improved teams, which more properly represent society and have fostered a healthier atmosphere for competitive endeavors. This demonstrates that when all aspects of the population are taken into consideration, everyone is served to their full potential.

As a source of motivation and advancement, pioneers such as Dawn Aponte, who is the chief football administrative officer for the NFL, and other women who have broken past the gender boundaries that exist within the league serve as guiding lights. Their experiences, which include overcoming skepticism and rejection, as well as successfully obtaining acknowledgment for their achievements, pave the path for future generations of women who will participate in football.

This is a mirror of larger cultural movements toward gender equality and inclusion, which can be seen in the changing environment of the NFL, which is characterized by the growing participation of women in significant capacities. It is not only the continued acceptance of diversity by the league that contributes to the enhancement of the game of football, but it also serves as a great example for other sectors and sports. A monument to the tenacity, ability, and dedication of the women who are redefining the NFL, the progress that has been made so far is a testament to the fact that the NFL is becoming a genuinely inclusive league.

To highlight the actual progress that is being made, the Browns have made a commitment to employing women from the NFL's Women's Forum, they have promoted Callie Brownson to the position of assistant coach, and they have received backing from prominent executives such as Kevin Stefanski and Dee Haslam. The NFL is not just a game for boys; it is a game for everyone. This is a strong message that the league is sending to young girls and women all around the world as it continues to embrace diversity and inclusiveness.

The NFL is still on its way to achieving gender equality, but the progress that has been accomplished in recent years cannot be denied. Through its advocacy of diversity and inclusiveness, the league is not only contributing to the improvement of the overall quality of the game, but it is also laying the groundwork for a future in sports that is more equal and inclusive. As trailblazers such as Rapoport, Raiche, and Aponte continue to motivate and guide, the NFL is on the verge of entering a new age, one in which women are not only players but rather vital components of the sport that is most cherished in the United States.

We've seen some very important examples of the fact that the NFL is passing through a period of change. There is a wave of increasing influence and presence of women in a field where female presence used to be marginal or even non-existent. The NFL is seeing a dramatic shift in the organization's dynamics, both on and off the field, as more women hold prominent roles inside the league.

Yet, even with these achievements in mind, the march toward gender equality in the NFL is not even close to being finished. Allegations ranging from gender discrimination to toxic environments in the workplace continue to surface, which is an indication that while there has been progress, there is still a significant amount of work to be done. The complicated issues that the league has as it aims for good progress for women are shown by the controversy that surrounded the choice of the Browns to sign quarterback Deshaun Watson, which occurred in the middle of allegations of sexual misbehavior.

Research on the Untold Journey of Women in American Football

Because of the predominately male viewpoint, the story of women's tackle football—one filled with fervor, tenacity, and an unwavering quest for recognition—remains mostly unsung in the annals of sports history. In spite of this, historian Russ Crawford's book *Women's American Football: Breaking Barriers On and Off the Gridiron* delves deeply into this little-known tale, highlighting the fierce passion and unwavering determination of women who have defied social expectations to leave their mark in a physically demanding and intense sport. This examination, written by an academic and writer who is well-versed in the culture around the sport, is a riveting account of women's steadfast dedication and innovations in American football, shedding attention on accomplishments that are starting to receive much-deserved acclaim.

The author's unplanned introduction to the vibrant world of women's contact football started in France when he discovered Les Sparkles de Villeneuve St. Georges, a squad founded by Sarah Charbonneau in 2011. This encounter—along with seeing the gripping Challenge Féminin championship in 2016—unveiled a thrilling, competitive sport that is mostly undiscovered by the general public but is comparable to men's football. He then began researching women's American football, exposing its fervent fan base and players' indisputable talent.

The 2017 Women's World Championship in Langley, British Columbia, proved to be a momentous occasion, demonstrating both the competitive nature of women's American football and its global reach. Throughout the competition, teams from all around the world showed off not just their physical prowess but also their sincere commitment to the sport. After seeing the United States of America's triumph in their third World Cup and Team Mexico's unexpected win over Great Britain, the author successfully encapsulated the essence of global competitiveness and the advancements made by women's football.

Inspired by curiosity and the thoroughness of a historian, the author set out on a lengthy quest to uncover the tales of women who had played American football with ardor. This project was not without its difficulties; it was intended to highlight the history of women in this fiercely competitive sport, which is frequently ignored. One major challenge was the dearth of historical records about women's football, which meant that oral histories from the players themselves were essential, with their individual experiences serving as the foundation for this investigation.

Leah Hinkle and Lea Kaszas were among the first to share their stories. Their perspectives not only showed the deep bond that women have with the game but also the international sisterhood created by their mutual love of football. Their stories started to create a clear image of a sport that, although it is primarily associated with men, exists in a parallel reality where women compete with equal passion and talent.

The author traveled to many games in both the US and Europe to add to the rich tapestry of women's American football history. Whether it was the heavily favored games in Columbus, Ohio, or the more evenly matched international contests, every game provided a different perspective on the state of women's tackle football as it exists now. The players' persistent zeal and tenacity highlighted their strong love for the game, while the differences in squad numbers and the effects of injuries highlighted the grassroots issues the sport faced.

These efforts culminated in a series of game observations and interviews that provided insight into a world where women have not only taken up tackle football with zeal but have also established supportive communities across continents. This was demonstrated by the author's contacts with the Suomen Amerikkalaisen Jalkapallon Liitto Ry in Finland and the Women's Football Alliance in the United States, which highlighted the resilience and friendship that define women's tackle football.

This investigation, which aimed to illuminate the accomplishments and challenges faced by female American football players, has become a monument to their unwavering determination. *Women's American*

Football sheds light on a piece of sports history that merits respect and acknowledgment through its thorough research and player biographies. In addition to highlighting these women's achievements, the author's trip and interviews serve as a call to recognize and encourage the contributions made by women to American football.

An important turning point in the recognition and appreciation of women's contributions to American football has been reached with the publication of *Women's American Football* by the University of Nebraska Press. This ground-breaking book challenges social standards and introduces readers to the commitment, talent, and passion of female athletes through an in-depth exploration of the underrepresented stories of women in sports. The author not only honors the accomplishments of these trailblazing women but also opens the door for upcoming generations of female players to pursue their goals on the gridiron by bringing attention to this frequently overlooked period of sports history.

But the story didn't finish when this book was published. Beyond the first volume, the author intends to continue this effort. A follow-up that will highlight the experiences of female American football players abroad and the sport's influence and worldwide reach is already planned. The author also plans to keep writing about important occasions, such as the IFAF World Cup Competition in Finland, to chronicle the development of women's American football.

In addition to adding to the historical record, this ongoing endeavor to bring attention to the accomplishments of women in American football hopes to encourage female players in the next generations to take up the sport. The author intends to promote a deeper understanding of the diversity and complexity of American football by bringing attention to an underappreciated facet of sports and encouraging a wider acknowledgment of women's contributions to the game.

The book *Women's American Football* is a celebration of progress, tenacity, and the unwavering spirit of women who have dared to question the status quo rather than merely a historical narrative. This book is a monument to the strength of desire and perseverance as the tale of women's tackle football develops. It serves as a reminder of past setbacks and victories as well as a ray of hope for what can be accomplished in the future.

In addition to telling the untold tales of women in a male-dominated sport, the book *Women's American Football* also acts as a guide for upcoming female athletes. With its release, a major step toward acknowledging and celebrating the contributions made by women to American football has been taken. The author challenges social standards and asks readers to reevaluate their ideas of gender roles in sports by exploring the history, struggles, and victories of female athletes.

Personal testimonies from players add depth to the story by showing their tenacity in the face of adversity and their will to succeed in a field dominated by men. These tales highlight how crucial it is to provide women in athletics equal visibility, encouragement, and chances. The book is a monument to the advancement, tenacity, and unwavering spirit of women who have dared to break the mold and carve out a position for themselves in American football.

The author intends to continue bringing attention to this frequently overlooked area of sports history in the future. There are plans to publish a second book that will concentrate on women who play American football abroad and continue covering events such as the

IFAF World Cup Competition in Finland. In addition to chronicling the history and accomplishments of female players in American football, this ongoing endeavor hopes to encourage female athletes in the coming generations to take up the sport.

The publication of *Women's American Football* and the upcoming initiatives highlight how women's involvement in sports is changing. The writer seeks to promote a more welcoming and equal athletic community by highlighting the breadth and depth of women's contributions to American football. By defying social norms and creating a space where women may compete, succeed, and inspire on the gridiron, the pioneering players' stories serve as a potent reminder of what can be accomplished when passion and tenacity unite.

In summary, *Women's American Football* celebrates the ground-breaking accomplishments of female athletes in a typically masculine sport and is more than just a history and interview compilation. This book serves as a landmark that not only chronicles the experiences of female players but also advances the subject of gender parity in sports as the story of women's tackle football develops. A new generation of players and fans will be inspired and encouraged by the dynamic and developing tale of women's American football thanks to the author's efforts, guaranteeing that the legacy of these trailblazing women will go on.

CHAPTER 10:

Empowering the Next Generation

—◆—

This book is about American football, but as we did in the chapter about World War II, it is useful to look for a while abroad and see what's happening at the international level with football (soccer). Similar to in the United States, it has traditionally been associated with men and considered not suitable for women, while other team sports, such as volleyball, were more accessible to female players.

Nevertheless, during the last years, a profound transformation has taken place in international women's football, which has gone from being marginalized to being a strong force in sports, with growing audiences and interest. Women's football is developing into an example of empowerment and a stage for promoting the overcoming of limiting gender conventions within the sports industry.

Female players have time and again proven their skill, determination, tireless dedication, and love for the game, proving their playing quality on the field. That has gained them respect, and their performances have not only raised the bar for competitiveness but have also opened the way for more media attention, sponsorship, and involvement on an international scale. This exposure, and mainly the quality of the product, has been very helpful in modifying perspectives and attitudes and attracting a devoted fan base, often from people who used to underestimate and contempt women's football. The sport is becoming increasingly appealing.

Extraordinary football players include Megan Rapinoe, Marta Vieira da Silva, and Sam Kerr. These women have inspired many people and become examples of empowerment and a preemptive attitude. This attitude helps cultivate a belief system among young women that goes beyond sports goals and encourages them to become agents of change and progress within their communities in general. Great athletes can be critical as role models.

In the pursuit of gender equality in the realm of sports, there has been a deliberate push to offer female athletes equal chances and resources. The implementation of grassroots initiatives, coaching programs, and improved access to facilities are all indications of a commitment to cultivating an environment that is conducive to the development of athletic potential in the future. In order to guarantee the continued development and vitality of women's football, these initiatives are of the utmost importance.

In addition, the fact that football intersects with other areas, such as betting advice, highlights the sport's broad appeal. Platforms that provide analyses and advice, such as the Smart Betting Guide, improve the engagement experience and appeal to a wider user base. This reflects the changing nature of the way fans connect with the sport, which demonstrates the sport's developing impact.

There is no possible way to overestimate the significance of FIFA's contribution to promoting women's football. The governing body of the sport has made it possible for female athletes to compete on a global platform by organizing high-profile competitions such as the

FIFA Women's World Cup. This has been a crucial factor in the sport's rise to popularity. The continuous funding and promotional efforts of FIFA are essential to the continuation of the momentum that has been driving the growth of women's football internationally.

In spite of the progress that has been accomplished, problems like salary inequality, unequal portrayal in the media, and widespread stereotypes continue to exist. Consistent campaigning and collective effort are necessary to address these concerns and guarantee that women's football will continue to progress. The relevance of representation is of the utmost importance; as more young women become aware of the opportunities available in football, the sport's attractiveness and degree of inclusion are sure to increase.

The triumph of women's football is, in essence, a symbol of a larger movement that is tearing down boundaries and opening new horizons. Not only does it represent athletic accomplishment, but it also represents the creation of a legacy that will empower and provide opportunities for future generations.

The sport's effect goes well beyond the playing field, ushering in a new age of equality and acknowledgment for women in football. As the sport continues to win hearts and inspire ambitions, its influence is expanding into new areas. Women's football is a cornerstone of empowerment and inclusion, and the road that lies ahead is full of potential milestones and accomplishments that will further reinforce its position as a cornerstone.

Providing Girls With the Means to Achieve Success and Improve Their Well-Being Through Sports

Sports have always had a crucial and beneficial role in the socio-cultural development of boys and men, as they provide numerous advantages that go from physical well-being and health to character growth and maturation. Sports have been shown to be an invaluable resource for individuals. Thus, it is of the utmost importance that we provide our girls with the same possibilities that we have provided for boys so that they, too, may experience the benefits that come with participating in sports. The fact that involvement in sports helps girls and women enjoy health improvement and psychological well-being and provides skills and abilities helpful for their future occupations and careers makes it obvious that this effort is crucial for society as a whole.

In 1974, legendary tennis player Billie Jean King formed the Women's Sports Foundation to empower girls through sports and physical exercise. The foundation's ultimate purpose is to promote access to the psychological, physiological, and sociological advantages of sports engagement for girls and women. While the Foundation's primary emphasis is on providing equal participation opportunities for female students at educational institutions, its ultimate objective is to facilitate access to these benefits.

Research has proven that sports participation for high school girls offers a number of benefits that one might not immediately associate with sports. Indeed, high school girls who are active in sports have a lower risk of undergoing unwanted pregnancies, they graduate from high school more often than their colleagues who are not involved in sports activities, and they also have better academic prospects (Oster, 2024). Regular physical exercise lowers substantially in women the risk of breast cancer and osteoporosis, research has shown (National Cancer Institute, 2020). It's important to add that this happens even in the case of minimal exercise time, as low as four hours per week.

Sports have a crucial positive role in enhancing well-being and long-term health.

It's evident that participating in athletics has a very beneficial impact on the psychological health and well-being of women, fostering self-esteem, confidence, and resilience, on top of the obvious positive impact on the body's health. Involvement in physical exercise and sports equips girls with skills that can be very useful and helpful on their path through adolescence and into adulthood. These skills include the development of skills, the setting of goals, and the opportunity to work together. Additionally, females who engage in athletics have a greater likelihood of developing a better body image and experiencing reduced levels of depression, all of which contribute to an overall improvement in mental health.

Additional to the well-being of the person, sports are an essential component in the process of training young women for success in the professional world. Boys have traditionally gained qualities that are needed for succeeding in the highly competitive corporate world via participation in athletics. Working together as a team, establishing goals, and behaving in an achievement-oriented manner are some of these abilities. An amazing 80% of the women CEOs who are included in Fortune 500 businesses said that they were tomboys at younger ages and participated in sports. This demonstrates that women are fast advancing to leadership positions in corporate America, and the experiences that they are able to bring to the table as former athletes provide them with a significant advantage.

There are still a substantial number of young women who face challenges in terms of access and opportunity within the realm of sports, despite the fact that there are obvious benefits associated with participation in sports. At least to a certain extent, the perpetuation of gender inequalities in sports is due to the fact that the culture of the field is dominated by what they call the male paradigm of organizational structure, which excludes or limits access to women. However, current tendencies toward gender equality and society's effort to implement it render it almost mandatory to work on removing similar limits and obstacles and, on the contrary, secure an inclusive setting where women will have the chance to flourish.

In summary, girls' empowerment through participation in sports is not only about improving their performance in a strictly athletic sense. It is crucial for their well-being and health and can help them have a fulfilling life. That's why investing in sports programs that can help girls and women unleash their full potential is important for society as a whole. This will result in a future that is brighter and more equitable for everyone.

Lessons That Are Crucial for Girls to Learn in Order to Achieve Success in Life

It has been known for a long time that sports are strong platforms that may be used to teach essential life lessons, inculcate critical skills, and nurture personal growth. Recognizing and developing ways to handle the precise obstacles and chances that female athletes can meet in the sports industry is extremely important. By teaching and helping our girls to embrace knowledge on these issues, they will be given more opportunities to succeed in the field of sports, which is often attractive, especially to young people, and can provide financial and professional potential. This will provide them with the skills they need to be successful in all parts of life, including sports.

A clear line of command occurs in hierarchical organizations, such as many men's sports teams, with the head coach delivering commands that players are expected to obey. The above is an example of a better understanding of the dynamics at work in organizations. Women tend to function in more decentralized and collegial ways, cultivating connections and searching for consensus and collaboration, while men tend to focus on the results and the best way to achieve efficiency. Having similar characteristics in mind can be very useful in preparing boys and girls to acquire the necessary skills to operate successfully and prosper in various types of organizational structures.

- **Understanding the Difference Between Self-Worth and Performance:** Winning and losing are essential components of both life and sports. Understanding how to gracefully accept failure and enjoy wins in a modest manner is beneficial to the development of resilience and perspective in people. It is essential for girls, just as it is for boys, to comprehend that their value as a person is not contingent upon their success on the field or in the office. This understanding is essential for the development of a robust sense of self-esteem and resilience.

- **Accepting Pressure and Competitiveness:** Pressure, deadlines, and competitiveness are all unavoidable components of both professional life and the world of sports. Athletes learn to thrive under pressure and consider competition as thrilling rather than daunting when they are given the opportunity to experience these difficulties in an atmosphere that is supportive or encouraging. Providing females with the opportunity to engage in athletics enables them to develop the self-assurance and resiliency that are necessary for success in contexts that are competitive.

- **Unlocking Resilience and Determination:** Hard effort, endurance, and determination are essential life lessons that people may learn by participating in sports. Athletes learn to draw from their inner stores of strength and perseverance, even when they are confronted with tiredness or hardship, and they push themselves to achieve victory. Girls who have a strong work ethic are equipped with the attitude necessary to overcome challenges and accomplish their objectives. This work ethic is easily transferable to other aspects of life.

- **The Pursuit of Excellence by Painstaking Attention to Detail:** Excellence may be attained through improving one's performance on a consistent basis and paying close attention to the details. In order to achieve excellence in every facet of their game, athletes focus on methodically studying their opponents, analyzing their own performance, and striving for perfection. Girls are able to acquire the abilities essential for success in sports and other areas of life by adopting a mentality that places an emphasis on constant learning and progress.

The Contribution of Role Models and the Importance of Encouragement

In spite of the fact that girls are becoming more interested in sports, they often do not get the same degree of encouragement and support as males. It is essential to provide girls with positive reinforcement, access to sports equipment, and exposure to female athletes as role models in order to cultivate their interest in sports and their confidence in their ability to participate in sports. We provide young girls the ability to pursue their athletic goals and reach their full potential by encouraging them to develop a love for athletics from a young age.

In conclusion, the lessons that are taught via involvement in sports extend well beyond the playing field, transforming participants into people who are resilient, resolute, and confident. In order to equip girls with the skills and mentality necessary to be successful in all aspects of life, we provide them with the tools to engage in athletics and access to surroundings that are encouraging. It is vital that we continue to raise awareness about the importance of girls participating in sports, that we recognize their accomplishments, and that we give them the support and role models they need in order to flourish. We have the ability to work together to build a future in which every girl has the chance to strive for excellence and achieve her ambitions of becoming an athlete.

Navigating the Complex Landscape of Youth Sports for Female Athletes

In the arena of child sports, the path of young female athletes is characterized by a distinct collection of obstacles and problems that go beyond the confines of the playing field. These difficulties, which are firmly based in sociological, economic, and cultural settings, have a key influence in determining the landscape of sports participation for girls and women in the United States. Financial difficulties are one of the most important impediments.

Expenses Incurred For Participation

The load of financial responsibility that comes along with participating in sports is a tremendous obstacle for a significant number of young athletes. The prices have a major influence on boys' and girls' accessibility to sports. Costs like the necessary equipment and training or traveling with the team can be very discouraging in some cases when kids come from low-income families. Moreover, the affirmation of a system of pay-to-play, that is, where the families have to cover the expenses of the kids' participation in sports outside and after school, further increases the financial problems they may face in supporting kids who want to be involved in sports activities. Despite the fact that this approach has not been generally embraced throughout states, it has resulted in inequities in access to chances for sports participation, especially among those who come from homes with lower incomes.

Choosing Between Early Entry and Specialization: A Catch-22

There is a considerable correlation between the age at which youngsters begin their involvement in sports and the level of commitment they maintain throughout time. Research indicates that females are more likely to begin their adventure in athletics later than boys, with early admission rates differing dramatically across various racial and cultural groups when compared to one another. This late start is compounded by the trend toward early specialization in a single sport, which is a practice that is frequently believed to be the path to elite status but has been criticized for its potential to narrow the opportunity for broad-based participation and may increase the risk of injury and burnout among young athletes.

Constrained Time and Competing Priorities Are Also Factors

The struggle between females' athletic pursuits and other life responsibilities, such as working, going to school, and maintaining relationships, becomes more intense as they get older. When compared to boys, girls are more likely to quit sports due to time restrictions, which is a significant element that drives this phenomenon. The difficulty of juggling the demands of their sport with the demands of their academics and other elements of life is not something that is exclusive to teenage athletes; even female collegiate players deal with this obstacle.

The Significance of Having a Supportive Environment and the Role That Expertise Plays in Coaching

It is impossible to exaggerate the impact that coaches have on the personal and social development of young female athletes. There is a positive, mastery-oriented environment that may be created by coaches who have received specialized education and training. This environment supports personal progress and continuous engagement in sports. On the other hand, the absence of competent coaches might be a barrier for young women who want to continue participating in sports.

Technology and a Sedentary Lifestyle

An additional obstacle to sports participation is the sedentary habits associated with increasing technology usage. This is especially true in an era dominated by screens. Young girls are competing for their time and attention with the appeal of social media and video games, which may have the potential to distract them from their participation in sports and other forms of physical exercise.

In Order to Go Forward, We Must Address the Obstacles

It is vital to take a multi-pronged strategy in order to increase the percentage of young girls who participate in sports and to guarantee that they will continue to be engaged in sports far into adulthood. Among them are the elimination of financial obstacles via the provision of scholarships and more egalitarian approaches to finance, the promotion of involvement in several sports rather than early specialization, and the guarantee of the availability of coaches who are both competent and helpful. Additionally, the creation of surroundings that are safe and accessible for sporting activities, in conjunction with attempts to strike a balance between the use of technology, may result in the creation of places that are more welcoming and inclusive for young female athletes to flourish in.

Achieving more equality and inclusion for girls in the field of young athletes' sports is an ongoing process. The wish would be for organizations and institutions to acknowledge and find solutions to those problems so they can set the way for every girl to have the chance to participate in sports in the future and to achieve her athletic dreams, above all, to gain the beneficial impact sports have on all aspects of life.

Obstacles to the Participation of Girls and Women in Extracurricular Activities

The involvement of girls and women in sports is determined by a multitude of interrelated obstacles that go beyond simple personal choice. This is the case in the changing environment of sports. Recent research and insights provide a comprehensive examination of these problems, bringing to light the multidimensional character of the problem that is now being addressed.

Technology and Lifestyle Are at the Intersection of the Two

There is a significant impact that various forms of technology have on the lifestyle choices that young females make. An investigation conducted by Sackett et al. (2018) with the participation of members of a Girl Scout Troop indicated that the widespread availability of electronic devices and social media had a considerable influence on the participants' propensity to engage in physical activities that take place outside. The appeal of engaging in sports is often overshadowed by the allure of the digital world, which is indicative of a broader trend in society toward indoor leisure activities.

The Struggle Against Gender Stereotypes and Norms

The environment of American sports is considered to often dissuade women's participation due to rigid rules and discriminatory attitudes, despite the most recent trends. Female athletes may be talented but are sometimes challenged by this kind of cultural assumption and are subjected to excessive examination and evaluation, critics say. On the other hand, continuous evaluation is inherent in sports, and that's what they are all about: constant competition and the need to perform in order to go on. Anyway, the fight against prejudices that can result in unjust limitations is a continuing effort for female athletes who are attempting to find their way in the sports industry.

The Constraints of Finances Are a Significant Obstacle

There is a significant barrier in the form of financial constraints that prevents girls and women from participating in sports. The shift toward pay-for-play models in school sports, in conjunction with the rapidly increasing expenses involved with participation, creates a tremendous strain on families, especially those who come from homes with lower incomes. This economic difficulty is made much more difficult for girls who come from minority groups. These girls often find themselves at a disadvantage as a result of structural injustices and a lack of resources.

Constrained Time and Competing Priorities Are Also Factors

It is difficult for female athletes to balance their personal lives, academic pursuits, and athletic endeavors. Research findings reveal that as females age, they tend to have fewer opportunities to participate in sports since they have to balance other responsibilities, such as school and job obligations (Women's Sports Foundation, 2020). As a result of this tendency, there is an increased need for positive surroundings that promote equilibrium and make it easier to participate in sports for an extended period of time.

A Look at the Importance of Support and Coaching Systems

The quality of coaching and the formation of an environment that is supportive and focused on mastery are of the utmost importance in creating good developmental gains for female athletes. A knowledgeable and experienced coaching staff is positively correlated with practice encouragement and improved athletic experiences, both of which impact girls' continued participation in sports.

Managing Multiple Identities While Meeting the Expectations of Different Cultures

When it comes to the experience of engaging in sports, the intersectionality of gender with cultural, ethnic, and socioeconomic characteristics has a key role in shaping the experience of girls' and women's involvement. For many girls and women, participating in sports is particularly difficult because of cultural and religious expectations and limitations related to their identity, other than gender-based dynamics and teasing. Managing this kind of challenge is essential for a wide range of female aspiring athlete groups.

To Promote Participation in Sports That Is Both Inclusive and Equitable

A multidimensional strategy that takes into consideration the economic, social, and cultural aspects of the problem is required in order to accomplish the goal of removing the obstacles that prevent girls and women from participating in sports. Steps that are vital to leveling the playing field include the creation of fair access to sporting opportunities, the promotion of varied role models, and the cultivation of cultures that challenge gender stereotypes and encourage diversity.

Acknowledging and solving the specific problems that girls and women confront is essential for achieving greater equity in sports. Removing the obstacles that prevent them from participating can create a sports environment that is more welcoming and empowering for people of all backgrounds.

The Addressing of Concerns Regarding Health and Safety in Women's Sports

The world of sports provides female athletes with a plethora of advantages, ranging from the enhancement of their physical health to the facilitation of their personal growth and the formation of social ties that may last a lifetime. However, these advantages are accompanied by a wide range of health and safety problems that need to be effectively managed in order to guarantee the health and safety of female athletes.

Various Concerns Regarding Health and Safety in the World

Despite the fact that it is rewarding, participation in sports may present a number of concerns for one's health and safety. There are, of course, risks and dangers inherent in sports for anybody, such as injuries during the games or training, stress and psychological pressure created by the expectations of performance and good results, and the fact that victory and success can't be achieved by all. Then, there are rare but existent issues regarding the relations and behaviors of other athletes and coaches. Bullying or abuse unfortunately happens sometimes, and institutions should be aware in order to face them and, before that, to prepare young athletes for how to react and ask for support and help. The establishment of a secure and encouraging atmosphere for female athletes requires, first and foremost, an awareness of these vulnerabilities and the subsequent treatment of them.

What is the Power Structure of Coaching?

One of the basic characteristics of the interaction between a coach and an athlete is an imbalance of power. The dynamics of this relationship may sometimes result in abusive actions, such as verbal or emotional abuse, neglect, or bullying. The mental health of an athlete is not the only thing that may be negatively affected by these types of abuse; they can also cause the athlete to lose faith in the sports system, which may discourage them from participating. It has been shown by research that the authoritarian character of sports might produce an environment that is conducive to the maltreatment of athletes, which highlights the need to maintain attention and take preventive measures (Gattis C, Moore M., 2022).

Justification of the Unjustifiable

It's possible that some coaches would justify their abusive conduct by claiming that it's a kind of incentive or a protective precaution. The reasoning behind such conduct might obscure the negative consequences of such behavior, making it more difficult for athletes and spectators to identify and handle instances of abuse. It can be odd and certainly is a subtle operation to distinguish between "tough love," that is, pushing the athlete to reach and overcome their limits, and "outright mistreatment," which, with the pretext of preparing and helping the athlete, goes over the limit of acceptable standards of conduct, ending up in unethical behavior and abuse.

Regarding the Obstacles to Overcome

A strategy that takes into account a variety of factors is necessary in order to protect the health and safety of female athletes. This includes the following:

- **Education:** It is essential for raising awareness in athletes, coaches, and sports organizations by teaching them how to spot possible signs of abuse. They are also important for maintaining healthy and respectful relationships with athletes.
- **Support Systems:** It is of the utmost importance to have support systems that enable athletes to come forward with their problems without the fear of being punished. This includes procedures for anonymous reporting and assistance for athletes who are suffering abuse.
- **Policy and supervision:** To guarantee that their rules are followed, sports organizations need to ensure that they have clear policies against abuse supported by supervision measures. This entails providing coaches with consistent instruction on ethical conduct and the welfare of athletes.

It is vital to continue researching the incidence and impacts of coach abuse to better understand the magnitude of the problem and to create successful remedies. Open discourse may reduce the stigma associated with these concerns, which can also inspire more athletes to share their experiences.

To make progress in creating safer conditions for women to participate in sports, it is necessary to acknowledge the intricate relationship between health and safety problems and to take preventative measures to address these issues. By cultivating a culture that is characterized by respect, support, and responsibility, we can make certain that the sporting arena continues to serve as a place where all female athletes may experience positive growth and empowerment.

CONCLUSION

—◆—

The story of women's football tells the evolution of a sport from its humble beginnings as exhibition and local entertainment to the formation of professional and semi-professional leagues and the achievements of women who established themselves as protagonists at the higher levels of the sport. At the same time, as we've seen and mentioned several times in this book, the story of women's football, or more generally of women and American football, is one of the characteristic examples of broader societal transformation and efforts for equality and inclusivity.

Sports are like a magic mirror where social tendencies and conditions are represented in a much simpler and easier-to-understand way than in the broader society. The progress of women's football during the last historical period, despite its difficulties and shortcomings, and the growth of women's significance and role in the NFL, a fortress of masculinity that seemed unsuitable for women, and around it marks a significant development in gender roles and expectations.

Less than a century ago, people thought that having women in football was bad for masculinity and femininity alike, almost a danger to social stability and security. During the following decades, life greatly superseded those visions as societal development changed the perceptions of genders and women's roles in society. American football can be a symbol of this development, as being the one of the roughest team sports, and thus more correlated to a certain perception of masculinity, was the hardest one to follow societal development. Fortunately, today, almost nobody thinks that masculinity and femininity could be damaged because women play football or work for men's football leagues. However, old prejudices are not totally gone, and more challenges lie ahead.

Women's football is a story of trailblazers: women who defied societal expectations and stereotypes and pursued their goals and inclinations based on their talents and their will for hard work and achievement. On the one hand, their success has a social meaning: that people should not be judged on their gender or race but on their abilities and character. On the other hand, it points out that work ethic, persistence, and determination can overcome any obstacles and prejudices. There is disparity and inequality in the world, but there is also appreciation for those who try to work diligently and genuinely love what they do. Sometimes appreciation can come from directions one wouldn't consider, as people often change their minds due to excellent examples rather than empty words from politicians and journalists who, above everything, try to promote their own careers.

The remarkable women we mentioned in this book, and many more who play or operate in the American football and sports industry, even without any reward whatsoever, but only because of their love for the game, did not just stand there lamenting and asking for more opportunities. They went ahead, claiming what they thought could become theirs, and took it. They became examples and arguments in favor of equality with their actions and work, not advocates of "equality" looking to promote their interests through rhetorical activism. The latter can be beneficial only based on real examples and actions.

The women who acted, moved by their love for their sport, didn't know if they would succeed in becoming professional players or coaches, and most of them did not. Nevertheless, they all succeeded in doing what they loved, enriched their sport, and became examples for all of us. That could be the most important takeaway of the women's football story so far: an example of talent and love for the game, persistence, and resilience in the face of adverse conditions.

References

AbiRafeh, L. (2022, December 6). *The (in)compatibility of Feminism and Football*. Medium. https://linaabirafeh.medium.com/the-in-compatibility-of-feminism-and-football-c1cc4ff0cb58

Achenbach, E. (2023, November 21). *NFL's women revolutionize the game, take charge in key roles*. ClutchPoints. https://clutchpoints.com/nfls-women-revolutionize-game-key-roles

American women and World War II (article) | Khan Academy. (n.d.). Khan Academy. https://www.khanacademy.org/humanities/us-history/rise-to-world-power/us-wwii/a/american-women-and-world-war-ii

Amy Adams Strunk. (n.d.). Forbes. https://www.forbes.com/profile/amy-adams-strunk/

Amy Adams Strunk biography. (n.d.). Tennessee Titans. https://www.tennesseetitans.com/team/front-office-roster/amy-adams-strunk

Associated Press. (2023, February 28). *Bucs' Maral Javadifar, Lori Locust 1st female coaches to win Super Bowl*. NFL. https://www.nfl.com/news/bucs-maral-javadifar-lori-locust-1st-female-coaches-to-win-super-bowl

Banks, D. (2019, November 7). *Kathryn Smith, the NFL's first female full-time coach, is not thinking about history*. Sports Illustrated. https://www.si.com/nfl/2016/08/25/buffalo-bills-kathryn-smith-nfl-assistant-coach

Benefits - Why Sports Participation for Girls and Women. (2023, October 31). Women's Sports Foundation. https://www.womenssportsfoundation.org/advocacy/benefits-sports-participation-girls-women/

Bills hire Kathryn Smith, first full-time female coach. (2023, February 28). NFL. https://www.nfl.com/news/bills-hire-kathryn-smith-first-full-time-female-coach-0ap3000000626344

Booher, C. (2024, January 25). *Campbell: Sheila Hamp is "Unique", Lions' success her vision*. All Lions FanNation. https://www.si.com/nfl/lions/news/campbell-sheila-hamp-unique-lions-success

Boomer, L. (2023, January 21). *Post-War - Women & the American Story*. Women & the American Story. https://wams.nyhistory.org/confidence-and-crises/post-war/

Breaking The Lines. (n.d.). *The rise of women's football: Empowering the next generation of players*. Breaking the Lines. https://breakingthelines.com/opinion/the-rise-of-womens-football-empowering-the-next-generation-of-players/

Cersosimo, B. (2023, August 9). *Next Woman Up: Robin DeLorenzo, NFL official*. NFL. https://www.nfl.com/news/next-woman-up-robin-delorenzo-nfl-official

Crawford R. (2022). *Women's American football: breaking barriers on and off the gridiron*. University of Nebraska Press.

Crawford R. (2023, January 25). *The making of women's American football: breaking barriers on and off the field*. Sports History Network. https://sportshistorynetwork.com/football/womens-american-football-breaking-barriers-on-and-off-the-field/

Drury, S., Stride, A., Fitzgerald, H., Hyett-Allen, N., Pylypiuk, L., & Whitford-Stark, J. (2022). *"I'm a referee, not a female referee": the experiences of women involved in football as coaches and referees*. Frontiers in Sports and Active Living. https://doi.org/10.3389/fspor.2021.789321

Gattis C, Moore M. A conceptual analysis of maltreatment in sports: A sport social work perspective. Front Sports Act Living. 2022 Nov 3;4:1017308. doi: 10.3389/fspor.2022.1017308. PMID: 36406770; PMCID: PMC9669431.

Generation Equality Forum. (2024, March 18). Generation Equality Forum. https://forum.generationequality.org/

Gibbs, S. (2020, December 4). *Women's football and World War Two.* University of Wolverhampton. https://www.wlv.ac.uk/research/research-centres/centre-for-historical-research/football-and-war-network/football-and-war-blog/2020/womens-football-and-world-war-two/

Haislop, T. (2021, September 18). *Who is the NFL's female referee? Meet Sarah Thomas, the only woman official in the NFL in 2020.* Sporting News. https://www.sportingnews.com/us/nfl/news/nfl-female-referee-sarah-thomas/114uw3bkmy0001hecsxvualx4w

Hawkins, J. (2023, April 10). *The future of American Football: Top 10 emerging technologies revolutionizing the game.* American Football Today. https://www.americanfootballtoday.com/post/the-future-of-american-football-top-emerging-technologies-revolutionizing-the-game-2

Hickey, K. (2023, January 28). *Carlie Irsay-Gordon "heavily involved" in Colts interview process.* Colts Wire. https://coltswire.usatoday.com/2023/01/28/nfl-colts-carlie-irsay-gordon-head-coach-interview-heavily-involved-process/

Kleen, B. (2022, August 4). *"Every Day Gets Better": The rise of women in sports media.* Global Sport Matters. https://globalsportmatters.com/culture/2022/08/02/every-day-gets-better-rise-women-in-sports-media/

Maral Javadifar Bio, age, ethnicity, family, husband, Buccaneers, Super Bowl, salary. (2021, February 7). Facts Files. https://fact-files.com/maral-javadifar-wiki/

McDowell, J., & Schaffner, S. (2011). *Football, it's a man's game: Insult and gendered discourse in "The Gender Bowl."* Discourse & Society, *22*(5), 547–564. http://www.jstor.org/stable/42889776

National Cancer Institute. Physical activity and cancer fact sheet. (2020, February 10). https://www.cancer.gov/about-cancer/causes-prevention/risk/obesity/physical-activity-fact-sheet

NFL teams hiring women for prominent roles at increasing rate. (2023, November 22). Sports Business Journal.

https://www.sportsbusinessjournal.com/Articles/2023/11/22/nfl-women-hiring

Nichols, T. (2024, March 5). *How women's football trailblazers started a revolution.* Just Women's Sports. https://justwomenssports.com/reads/womens-tackle-football-growth-wfa-wnfc-lisa-king/

Nouri, N. (2021, February 5). *Making Super Bowl History: Iranian-American Coach Maral Javadifar.* KAYHAN LIFE. https://kayhanlife.com/authors/making-super-bowl-history-iranian-american-coach-maral-javadifar/

Oster, E. (2024, January 5). Do high school sports really reduce unplanned pregnancy? - ParentData. Emily Oster's ParentData. https://parentdata.org/high-school-sports-unplanned-pregnancy/

Prasad, A. (2022, May 5). *A level playing field: The past, present and future of women's football.* FanSided. https://fansided.com/2022/05/05/womens-football-past-present-future/

Russo, K. (2024, March 5). *Callie Brownson highlighted as one of 12 women coaches during the NFL Women's Forum.* Cleveland Browns. https://www.clevelandbrowns.com/news/callie-brownson-highlighted-as-one-of-12-women-coaches-during-the-nfl-women-s-forum

Sheila Ford Hamp biography. (n.d.). Detroit Lions. https://www.detroitlions.com/team/front-office-roster/sheila-ford-hamp

Sport for Generation Equality: advancing gender equality in and through sport. (2020, March 10). UN Women. https://www.unwomen.org/en/news/stories/2020/3/news-sport-for-generation-equality

Sports, World War II. (n.d.). Encyclopedia.com https://www.encyclopedia.com/defense/energy-government-and-defense-magazines/sports-world-war-ii

Strategy details. (2024, February 21). FIFA. https://inside.fifa.com/womens-football/strategy/strategy-details

Tran, D. (2022, December 29). *Michigan graduate assistant a trailblazer for female coaches*. NBC Sports. https://www.nbcsports.com/college-football/news/michigan-graduate-assistant-a-trailblazer-for-female-coaches

Unsworth, N. (2019, July 18). *The changing face of women's sports*. Inspiresport. https://www.inspiresport.com/the-changing-face-of-womens-sports/

Vega, A. (2024, January 17). *Who is Jim Irsay's daughter, Carlie?* The US Sun. https://www.the-sun.com/sport/10116175/who-jim-irsay-daughter-carlie-gordon/

Veliz P, Shakib S. (2014) Gender, Academics and Interscholastic Sports Participation at the School Level: A Gender-specific Analysis of the Relationship between Interscholastic Sports Participation and AP Enrollment. *Sociological Focus*. 47(2), 101-120. https://www.tandfonline.com/doi/abs/10.1080/00380237.2014.883849

Westly, E. (2023, December 6). *The forgotten history of women's football*. Smithsonian Magazine. https://www.smithsonianmag.com/history/forgotten-history-womens-football-180958042/

Williams, M. (2021, November 15). *Female coaches in the NFL: Meet two of the record-setting 12 women leading teams in 2021*. Sporting News. https://www.sportingnews.com/us/nfl/news/female-nfl-coaches-women-record/11ygnjw97krf91thjft3iryrg5

Withers, T. (2023, November 22). *In the NFL, more women than ever are rising in rank. Why now?* The Christian Science Monitor. https://www.csmonitor.com/USA/Society/2023/1122/In-the-NFL-more-women-than-ever-are-rising-in-rank.-Why-now

Whitlock, F. (2020, August 18). *American athletes and spectator sports during World War II*. Warfare History Network. https://warfarehistorynetwork.com/american-athletes-spectator-sports-during-world-war-ii/

Women's Sports Foundation (2020, January). *Chasing Equity: The Triumphs, Challenges, and Opportunities in Sports for Girls and Women.* A Women's Sports Foundation Research Report.

Yang, A. (2020, January 22). *49ers' Katie Sowers first female, openly gay coach in Super Bowl history.* Sports Illustrated. https://www.si.com/nfl/2020/01/22/katie-sowers-first-female-openly-gay-coach-super-bowl

Printed in Great Britain
by Amazon